Social Change Philanthropy in America

Alan Rabinowitz

Foreword by
David R. Hunter

QUORUM BOOKS

New York
Westport, Connecticut
London

Library of Congress Cataloging-in-Publication Data

Rabinowitz, Alan.
    Social change philanthropy in America / Alan Rabinowitz ; foreword
by David Hunter.
        p. cm.
    Includes bibliographical references.
    ISBN 0–89930–536–9 (lib. bdg. : alk. paper)
        1. Charities—United States.   2. Endowments—United States.
    3. Social change.   I. Title.
    HV91.R33   1990
    361.7'0973—dc20   89–24362

British Library Cataloguing in Publication Data is available.

Library of Congress Catalog Card Number: 89–24362
ISBN: 0–89930–536–9

First published in 1990

Quorum Books, 88 Post Road West, Westport, CT 06881
An imprint of Greenwood Publishing Group, Inc.

Printed in the United States of America

(∞)

The paper used in this book complies with the
Permanent Paper Standard issued by the National
Information Standards Organization (Z39.48–1984).

10 9 8 7 6 5 4 3 2 1

SOCIAL CHANGE PHILANTHROPY IN AMERICA

For Andrea

Contents

Figures and Tables   ix

Foreword by David R. Hunter   xi

Preface   xv

Part One. Philanthropy and Social Change

   1.   Introduction to the Network of
       Funders and Grantees   3

   2.   The Philanthropic Universe   13

   3.   The Flow of Philanthropic Dollars   25

Part Two. A Portrait of Social Change Funders

   4.   The Emergence of the Progressive
       Social Change Network   37

   5.   How Social Change Funders Think
       about Their Work   53

Part Three. A Portrait of Social Change Grantees

6. Definitions of a Social Change
    Grantee   73

7. A Typology of Social Change
    Grantees   81

Part Four. Risk Analysis and the Funding Decision

8. How Funders Make Their Decisions   99

9. How Funders Evaluate Their Work   109

10. Stabilizing the System   117

Part Five. Politics and Prospects

11. Populism and the Foundation
    World   133

12. People and Prospects for the 1990s   145

    *Appendix: Analysis of Prototypical
    Project Grants*   157

    Notes   205

    Select Bibliography   217

    Index   221

Figures and Tables

FIGURES

2.1   Money Flows in the Philanthropic
        System   17

7.1   CHD Grants: Total and Social
        Development, 1980–1987   90

7.2   CHD Grants by Technical Category,
        1980–1987   91

10.1   General Support for CIS, 1954–1988   118

TABLES

3.1   Independent Sector Revenues, 1984   26

3.2   Analysis of Private Foundations   28

3.3   Funding by Religious Organizations, 1988 32

5.1   Distribution of Funding Sources in *The
        Grantseekers Guide*   66

7.1   Distribution of 1,482 Grants by Subject   86

7.2   Distribution of Grants by State   87

7.3   Analysis of Projects Funded by CHD,
        1980–1987   89

7.4   Distribution of CHD Grants by Subject
           and Ethnic Group, 1986–1987   92
11.1   Distribution of GOTV Funds, 1988
           Campaign   142

Foreword

The idea of philanthropy is a strong component of the American ethos. People are used to the idea of giving money to help others through churches or community red feather drives. Charity is seen as something that should be espoused by everybody. Philanthropy comes under the general rubric of charity. Tax laws refer to "charitable giving" as one of the things foundations are all about. But there are various approaches to philanthropy.

Philanthropy is not homogeneous in form or substance. Some swear by "bricks and mortar." Others by direct aid or services to the needy. Others by "institution building."

This book is about a category of philanthropy that hasn't yet been definitively limned: social change philanthropy. How does it differ from "traditional" philanthropy?

The essential difference is that social change philanthropy aims explicitly to facilitate the changing of societal institutions so they don't produce the very problems that "charity" tries to alleviate. While it is not possible to draw a clear and unequivocal line between traditional and social change philanthropy, and there is some overlap, it is possible to discern some distinctions between them.

Social change philanthropy tends to be more critical of existing social and economic arrangements in the society.

It tends to be more "activist." *Change* is seen as a transitive verb.

Social change philanthropy finds itself more involved with controversial and political affairs (correction: it doesn't "find" itself there—it goes there).

In what is almost an article of faith it insists that the beneficiary communities have a strong role in allocating contributed funds.

It concerns itself more with questions of power—who has it, how you get it if you don't have it, how it is made consonant with democratic principles, how it can be more equitably distributed throughout the society.

It is less afraid of the term *fundamental change* than are more traditional philanthropies.

It tends to come in smaller packages. In the totality of philanthropic resources it is miniscule.

It is more often deployed by donors as one instrument in association with other vehicles for social action, such as electoral activity, volunteer work, research, and writing. In consequence it is less institutional and bureaucratic.

This book brings these generalizations to life in a thorough analytic catalogue. The information pulled together here will be useful for academic observers and students of American society. But perhaps of even greater importance it will serve as a recruitment or mobilizing device. It shows progressive wealthy individuals and progressive church groups that there are imaginative ways of promoting public policy that imply fundamental transformation of some of the institutions that determine our individual and collective well-being.

It shows that there are others out there acting through their wealth to make a better society and to promote unselfconsciously humanistic and democratic values—the values Frances Moore Lappe highlights in her book *Rediscovering American Values*: freedom, fairness, and democracy.

The casual observer may be unaware that deploying resources in the ways described in this book can have an exhilarating and invigorating effect on the donor. It is exhilarating to be seriously engaged in common effort to make a better world and to have the wherewithal to play a significant role.

This book is about more than just progressive social change

philanthropy. In a way, it looks at some of the contours of American society through the window of social change philanthropy. It puts its subject in context. To follow the action in philanthropy requires going into a vast array of "problem areas." This book does a comprehensive job of that. It is a portrait of a country from a particular vantage point painted with objective and sympathetic strokes. And it is readable.

It should be read by an audience far beyond those directly engaged in philanthropic activity.

—David R. Hunter

Preface

Everyone agrees that the 1990s will be a stressful time for philanthropy generally, for our economy is fragile, there are continuing uncertainties about the impact of tax legislation on giving patterns, and social needs have increased at a frightening pace. Confident that their programs are effecting significant long-term improvements in conditions, the funders and grantees that comprise the progressive social change community will be under great pressure to maintain existing sources of funds, to expand the number of donors, and to deal with the rising expectations that giving programs generate.

My most compelling objective in writing this book is to broaden the public's understanding of how progressive social change philanthropists think and operate. A slightly less impelling motive is to provide donors and grantees already committed to progressive activism with a fresh and comprehensive view of the institutional environment in which they work.

Insiders in the field of progressive social change philanthropy were my primary sources for the writing of this book, the first study of their work in the context of philanthropy generally. I hope this book is also read by those "traditional" foundation trustees, professional staffers, and ordinary people who, up to now, have tended to look cautiously and even suspiciously at grants to empower disadvantaged groups in our society.

Almost all Americans, rich and poor, are philanthropists, giving their money and their time to a bewildering variety of causes and institutions. I have the highest praise for the many constructive, even innovative, nonprofit institutions and public-interest campaigns that Americans create. The pluralism, diversity, and electoral politics that are America's pride provide each citizen with a wide choice of worthy causes to support.

I focus here, however, on philanthropy for "progressive social change," never better defined than by David Hunter in his foreword to this book. As Hunter says, social change philanthropy aims to change societal institutions so that they do not produce the problems traditional charity tries to alleviate. Our mutual interest is the work of an increasing number of funders to empower low-income and minority groups to improve their social and economic position in American society. Some of the funders I surveyed prefer to support local grass-roots organizing efforts. Some prefer to support policy-formulating think tanks and national compaigns concerning issues involving the environment, children, health, peace, and on through the long list of possible categories. Some fund across the entire spectrum of opportunities.

Meanwhile, social scientists are just beginning to document and analyze the vast nonprofit sector of the American economy, to record the activities of the major foundations, and to categorize the hundreds of thousands of charitable and educational organizations that are the beneficiaries of the American public's philanthropic impulses. By comparison, documentation and data concerning the past three decades of progressive social change philanthropy are sorely lacking, and my research is thus a beginning upon which future archivists and historians can expand.

"Philanthropoids," as observers of the philanthropic scene are called, still lack academically acceptable models of "mainstream" philanthropy that are capable of predicting either inputs of resources or outcomes under constantly changing political and economic conditions. Important and enduring social changes have occurred in the past three decades. The progressive social change community of funders and their activist grantees emerged during this period, but their efforts are even less well documented and evaluated than those of the more traditional charities. Given the broad spectrum of social activism that characterizes the American culture, the examples, data, and quotations woven into my text are only representative of a greater whole, and my findings become "currently useful generalizations" as America moves into its uncharted future. The philanthropic scene changes constantly as current events become history.

In the future, as in the past, the system of progressive social change philanthropy I describe will require a supply of funders with some common views regarding the need to strengthen participatory democracy; a number of individuals able to articulate and initiate programs of national or local importance; and a very large number of volunteers and professional staffers to implement programs, with attendant lawyers, accountants, and other functionaries.

While my research methodology is consistent with some of the social science research methods I learned in earning my Ph.D. at MIT, I make no pretense here at conceptionalizing a cohesive behavioral model. Yet, bit by bit, as I talked with my knowledgeable sources and read the published and unpublished materials they supplied or suggested, the elements of the dynamic system that engaged their energies took form as the five parts of this book.

Part One sets the scene. Chapters 1 and 2 are an introduction to the network of progressive social change funders and grantees in the context of America's political economy and its philanthropic institutions. Chapter 3 is an analysis of the flow of dollars through the entire nonprofit system, leading to an original estimate of funds disbursed annually to social change grantees.

Part Two is a portrait of social change funders. Chapter 4 is the product of my research into the history of progressive social change philanthropy. Chapter 5 is my review of recent studies of how both religious leaders and wealthy individuals think about philanthropy and social justice, with a concluding section on where such funders can be found.

Part Three focuses on the grantees. Chapter 6 discusses the criteria employed by leading funders in identifying and selecting

appropriate projects for funding. Chapter 7 contains my typology of grantees and my analysis of 1,482 grants actually made
in recent years by six representative funders: the U.S. Catholic
Conference's Campaign for Human Development, the Youth
Project, Joint Foundation Support, and the Tides, Threshold,
and Women's Foundations. This analysis of actual project grants
provides empirical evidence of the characteristics of successful
applicants.

Are grants for progressive social change worthwhile? Effective? Are grantees sufficiently accountable? Are funders and
grantees meeting each other's needs? Part Four, entitled "Risk
Analysis and the Funding Decision," takes up these questions.
Chapter 8 shows how funders make their decisions and try to
improve the effectiveness of their grant-making and the accountability of grantees. Chapter 9 looks at how funders evaluate
the worthwhileness of their work and passes on the valedictory
comments of David Hunter, the retiring dean of progressive
funders. Chapter 10 considers through examples funding questions from the viewpoint of grantees trying to establish long-
term relationships with funders in order to improve the structure
of the field as well as to increase the chances of their own survival.

Part Five is an exploration of progressive funding as an arena
of controversy, conflicting ideologies, and, ultimately, electoral
politics. Chapter 11 tackles the political history of the field, with
commentaries on changing tax codes and on the direct and indirect methods used by progressive funders to support voter
registration and issue-based campaigns in the 1980s. Chapter 12
discusses challenges and prospects for the progressive social
change community as strategies for organizing, campaigning,
and fund-raising are developed for the future.

During my research, I encountered many prospective funders
who seemed to have no knowledge of progressive social change
philanthropy or whose perceptions of it were surprisingly narrow. Thus arose a need to illustrate in more detail the range and
substance of the work of progressive funding organizations in
order to expand understanding of the field and to stimulate
imagination. An annotated and classified collection of grants

made, notably by the Campaign for Human Development, is presented in the Appendix.

Numerous people gave me encouragement and usable material along the way to finishing this book. I am greatly indebted to the following knowledgeable folk (some "traditional" but most of them styling themselves as reasonably progressive) for listening, offering ideas and hard-to-find reports and papers, and, in some cases, giving my drafts a critical reading: Harriet Barlow, Anne Bartley, Richard W. Boone, Elizabeth Boris, Jim Browne, Robert Cabot, Don Elmer, W. H. Ferry, Barbara P. Fiske, Donald W. Fiske, Cynthia Guyer, Mary Hall, Chester Hartman, Don Hopps, David R. Hunter, Douglas Lawson, Eunice Letzing, Jeff Malachowsky, S. M. Miller, Bob Nicklas, Farley Peters, Drummond Pike, Andrea W. Rabinowitz, Michael Seltzer, Greg Tuke, and Murray Weitzman. My editor at Quorum, Eric Valentine, and Deborah Johnson with her word processor were also invaluable.

The errors and omissions are mine. The book is yours.

Part One

Philanthropy and Social Change

Introduction to the Network of Funders and Grantees

Overview

Throughout this book, I refer to an informal network of activist funders and their grantees. I try to make visible some of the lines of communication among the set of funders concerned with social and economic issues, the recipients of grants to encourage specific kinds of social change, and the rest of the philanthropic community.

Because no other book (so far as I know) provides a comprehensive overview of progressive social change philanthropy, I undertook the job of exploring its uncharted realm, assembling its scattered literature, and examining its precepts and practices so that I—and other grantees, funders, and interested onlookers—might understand its real role in the philanthropic world at a time when the larger foundation world is burdened with concerns about its own future.

As much as possible, I have interviewed experienced foundation executives, activist grant recipients, and individual donors to supplement what all concerned consider to be gaps or misleading clues in the written record of the field. The documents from which I have quoted selectively are fully representative, I believe, of sentiments expressed with equal eloquence and acuity in hundreds of other annual reports and professional writings for which no central depository yet exists. The chapter footnotes include a number of references to standard and not-so-standard sources that may be of use to readers wanting more information.

My approach is as descriptive, analytic, objective, and non-prescriptive as I can manage, although I personally hope that my efforts will broaden support for the progressive social change community. The result of my approach is a form of systems analysis—analyzing existing relationships between willing funders and earnest grantees in order to find out how the system works, rather than presenting statements as to what kinds of grant applications ought to be funded.

My first assumption is that my readers, even if they have been active in one or another corner of the field, have as little information about how progressive social change philanthropy fits into the general scheme of philanthropy as I did when I began this project. Thus the appropriate starting point is a careful look at how nontraditional grants seem to fit into the whole field of organized philanthropy in the United States.

In fact, everyone in the universe of nonprofit causes needs more knowledge about the role and prospects for philanthropic giving, and social activism is only a small part of that universe. No one yet knows the extent to which philanthropy in the United States will suffer in the long term from the decrease in tax rates enacted in the Tax Reform Act of 1986. Leaders such as Richard Lyman, former president of the Rockefeller Foundation, are less than sanguine about the future.[1] As a result of cuts in federal programs and the general increase in economic stress, the need for funds for traditional charitable and educational institutions has never been greater. It follows that the future of funding for progressive social change activities—advocacy of better national policies and the empowerment of low-income and minority people and their grass-roots organizations—is a matter of concern lest the momentum of three decades of experience be allowed to wane.

The large foundations have realized since their origins in the nineteenth century that their grants were meant to induce some form of social change, for example, higher educational standards, new forms of social legislation, or the wider use of scientific methods. For most philanthropists, however, social change is problematic, and they prefer that their dollars go to noncontroversial objects of charity. They shy away from what they call "social change advocacy."

Unfortunately, advocacy of social change is also carried on by those who want to foster more grass-roots democracy and greater responsibility on the part of American corporations and by the proponents of draconian regimens enforcing specific moral codes and rightist interpretations of American partriotism. My own preference—and the focus of this book—is unambiguously the more democratic or progressive end of the spectrum.

A broader understanding is needed, beyond acceptance of the symbiosis of philanthropy and social change, of why some funders believe in grants to encourage democratic reform and others do not. A number of recent studies, some described later in the book, explore the motivations of different types of philanthropists and attempt to explain the various types of grant-making that characterize each type.

For many reasons ranging from lack of information to strong convictions against the practice, funding of progressive social change activities is a relatively minor item on most philanthropic agendas. This book is my attempt at providing foundation executives with a fair appraisal of the state of the art and with useful working definitions of the ambiguous and often controversial terms *progressive, social change,* and *social justice* as applied in the context of more traditional forms of philanthropy and charity.[2]

In any case, every philanthropic act has some social objective, either explicit or implicit. While most philanthropists consider that their charitable, educational, and health-service grants promote social welfare and reflect the changing needs of society, grants explicitly designed to achieve social justice or to effect social change have a different connotation than the usual run of social-welfare contributions.

As a group, philanthropists live up to their dictionary description as lovers of mankind, but they are fairly traditional in their giving patterns. For example, the national survey for Independent Sector's report, "The Charitable Behavior of Americans," found that most of the charitable contributions that Americans take as deductions on their federal income tax returns go for the support of religious institutions, hospitals, private educational institutions, and a vast array of other worthy charitable causes.[3]

Charity is the part of traditional philanthropy that expresses love for mankind by helping the needy. Charitable dollars go for Christmas baskets and soup kitchens, hospital clinics, aid to victims of natural disasters, housing for aged and indigent people, and similar kinds of short-term relief. Other parts of the philanthropic realm are focused on long-term objectives. These long-term goals include general support of educational, health, cultural, and environmental/conservation institutions; endowment of research and teaching facilities at universities and think tanks; and funds for the construction of libraries, hospitals, and educational centers and for the acquisition of environmentally or historically significant land and buildings for public use and enjoyment.

Private philanthropy and volunteered services are essential underpinnings of the infrastructure of our urbanized society. While charity helps people in the short run and the rest of philanthropic funds are largely devoted to maintaining and expanding our basic service institutions, a smaller number of established charitable foundations, churches, and individuals are willing to fund organizations working for greater fairness in America.

Social justice funders are clearly charitable, in that they look for ways to improve conditions in the short term. Charity and philanthropy generally ameliorate and preserve the existing social order, but social change philanthropy entails the inherent risk of encouraging challenges to that order and its institutions. Progressive social change philanthropy is an unwieldy name to describe the activities of funders who want to use their money to help create a fairer, cleaner, safer, more democratic, poverty-free world, but it is the only name that seems to be in common use by its practitioners.

Some funding organizations use *social justice* and *social change* to describe their objectives, but other funders appear to shy away from these terms because they may suggest an unwanted degree of advocacy or political involvement. *Fairness* seems to be a more neutral, perhaps more acceptable, term, with the goals of fairness covering at least the following:

- Full enjoyment of Constitutional rights
- Fair access to jobs, education, and housing
- Fair access to health services and a healthy environment

But even achieving fairness involves some nontraditional effort on the part of philanthropists, for fairness almost always implies changes in public policies, which in turn will ultimately involve use of political power to achieve change.[4] At the very least, advancing the cause of fairness, or social justice, calls for a more direct focus on the conditions of relatively disadvantaged groups in society, such as minorities, women, the unemployed, farmers, and so on.

The progressive American social change philanthropists who are the subject of this book take the risk of being controversial as they try to empower disadvantaged people to make permanent improvements in their social and economic environments and in the basic institutions of our society that affect their lives. These funders believe that the best form of charity is helping people help themselves, with an emphasis on citizen-based grass-roots organizing.

However, according to the Bay Area Committee for Responsive Philanthropy's survey of forty-five local foundations in the late 1970s, "The foundation community as a whole is either hostile or indifferent to the need for social change funding." The committee found that, with only a few exceptions, "Bay Area foundations have failed to actively support organizations working for social change."[5]

Most of the books and articles written about grant-making and grantees in the realm of progressive social change do little more than help funders evaluate proposals and help grantees with fund-raising. These include Kim Klein's *Fundraising for Social Change* distributed by the Funding Exchange, Michael Seltzer's *Securing Your Organization's Future: A Complete Guide to Fundraising Strategies*, written for the Foundation Center, and several directories of amenable funding sources.[6]

One of the few recent books to argue for more systematic funding of grass-roots democracy is Robert Matthews Johnson's *The First Charity*. Johnson, with long exposure to the field as executive director of the Wieboldt Foundation, proclaims "Democracy has not been philanthropy's first charity, and it ought to be."[7] Johnson's book fills a void in the literature, providing the theoretical basis for grass-roots participation in a pluralistic democratic republic as well as a workable set of criteria for community organizations to follow. He also offers three detailed case studies and a good deal of guidance to neophyte funders on how to evaluate grant proposals.

While most foundations, religious organizations, and other nonpartisan tax-exempt educational organizations may not go as far as Johnson would like, those that are involved in progressive social change philanthropy provide essential support for grantees concerned about impediments (or threats) to civil liberties, economic well-being, minority rights (including citizenship and voter registration), health, and environmental safety (especially with regard to toxics and waste disposal). A network of progressive social change funders took shape in the late 1960s and is discussed in Chapter 4. While its present members represent only a tiny fraction of the philanthropic efforts in America, they provide millions of dollars each year for general support of grass-roots organizations and for training in strategic thinking, lobbying, fund-raising, staff development, and coalition-building. Academic research and continuing services to individuals are rarely funded.

An impressive amount of time and money is expended by these funding organizations to identify and encourage suitable recipients of their largesse.[8] The grant-making process is similar to those of the major foundations, the United Way funds, and even the National Institutes of Health: the process involves long debates concerning appropriate topics to be supported, lengthy competitive applications, and site visits and evaluations. Compared to mainstream organizations, however, the social change funders willingly accept a much greater uncertainty of outcome, given the relative instability of community-based groups and the topical nature of many of the issues pursued.

Philanthropy and the Political Economy

The progressive social change philanthropists are a miniscule part of the system by which Americans support their nongovernmental nonprofit institutions. What follows is my attempt to identify these progressive social change advocates within the nonprofit universe.

The philanthropic system in the United States is a set of networks that is a part of our whole social system, a part of our political economy. The philanthropic system reflects the implicit and explicit goals and policies of all of our individuals and institutions. It has its own mechanisms for turning these goals and policies into programs and projects and for evaluating the outcomes as part of the process of adapting its policies to new conditions.

The basic goals of the philanthropic system are necessarily broad, general, endemic, and persistent. The goals reflect concern for the general welfare, a desire for social and economic stability, and, perhaps, an abiding belief in our collective ability to make progress toward a better society. Individual goals are dominated by a general desire for social justice, although definitions of what constitutes fairness and equity differ.

Our institutional goals as a society are far more problematic but equally persistent. The debate as to what it means to be a republic and what the consequences of becoming a true democracy might be has raged from the very beginning of the American experiment, and our government remains more Hamiltonian than Jeffersonian. There is little on the general philanthropic horizon that will be allowed to constitute a threat to the ruling classes, and, indeed, much of organized philanthropy can be seen as a means to maintain the interests of such classes and to keep democracy within bounds.[9]

We have come a long way toward a more stable and equitable socioeconomic system since Marx wrote *The Communist Manifesto* with its thunderous phrase about the specter of communism haunting Europe. One hundred years later, the literature of political economy, exemplified by Joseph Schumpeter's *Capitalism, Socialism and Democracy*, was full of our disenchantments with both capitalism and socialism.[10] And currently, almost three-quarters of a century since the Russian Revolution, a new wave of disenchantment is rolling over the world. This quotation from Robert Heilbroner's 1989 article, "The Triumph of Capitalism," provides a realistic summary of present-day perceptions of the impact of the social and socialistic movements of the post–World War II world:

> Less than seventy-five years after it officially began, the contest between capitalism and socialism is over; capitalism has won. . . . Fears that capitalism will run out of things to do appear much less plausible than they did in the past. . . . By all indications we live in a period of extremely rapid scientific advance, part of which will very likely result in new commodity possibilities; and the rout of socialism itself opens up virgin territory to the extension of capitalist enterprise. . . .
> The last seven years have been a period of . . . worsening poverty and increasingly ill-distributed income at home: the economist Robert Hamrin has recently pointed out that in 1986 the top twenty per cent of all American households received 46.1 per cent of all pretax and pretransfer income, while the bottom twenty per cent received 3.8 per cent—income before taxes and transfers being the best way to show how raw market forces work. Thus our much-touted boom is also the period in which we have set an all-time American record for disparity of income. . . .
> The history of every democratic capitalist nation is one of a widening provision of "entitlements," over the nearly universal opposition of business, because from the viewpoint of government these measures have seemed necessary to retain and strengthen the fealty of its citizens. . . . The bone of contention is no longer the principle of entitlements but their reach and level.[11]

Entitlements and other transfer payments help narrow an ever-increasing gap between rich and poor.[12] Meanwhile, Heilbroner writes of the dominance, even in social democratic nations, of the universal class of "businesspersons," and the job that progressive social change philanthropists have taken on to strike some sort of balance between that class and the rest of the population.

Making our existing system more fair is more important to the social change philanthropists than moving society toward either a capitalism completely dominated by the market or a socialism completely dominated by governmental agencies (or, as John B. Judis writes, "The abiding alternatives are not capitalism and communism, but democratic capitalism and a mature socialism tempered by experience and inoculated against one-party rule").[13] Nevertheless, the participants in this special brand of philanthropy seem to share strong feelings about the inequalities generated by our present mixed economic system, they value the positive roles that governmental powers and monies can play in reducing economic and social disparities, and, to improve the way capitalism operates, they encourage the growth of cooperatives and worker-owned-and-managed enterprises in low-income communities. The political objectives of the progressive social change philanthropists include greater respect for the U.S. Constitution and passage of reformist legislation, neither of which would alter the basic governmental framework of the United States.

Each of us learns his or her social policies from the culture in which we grow up—some of us stay close to our native culture, some of us change our ideas as we mature. Some people, perhaps, never are taught the concept of charity or the basic precepts of their responsibilities to their community or their fellow human beings, but I like to assume that practically everyone has a touch of philanthropy in his or her character and that we are not doomed to become a nation of narcissistic, hedonistic, solipsistic, amoralists. In fact, America's system of private philanthropic endeavors and broad participation in community affairs is more developed, and more necessary, than in any other nation.

The Philanthropic Universe

Philanthropic Policies

Regardless of their politics, Americans seem to have adopted remarkably similar policies by which to express their philanthropic instincts. Our gifts of money and time, beyond the demands for charity at moments of distress, are ordinarily targeted on one or more of the following "traditional" objectives:

- Making others more effective, by providing for better education and living conditions
- Supporting research that can be translated into better socioeconomic policies or better health conditions
- Providing facilities and general support for organizations whose activities we approve

The policies of those who want social change go a little further into the world of politics, both left and right of the aisle, but as Robert Johnson cautions:

Outsiders with strong political inclinations sometimes look to community organizations for grass-roots confirmation of their own convictions. Politically progressive activists will suggest that community groups join in advocating a whole new American system with massive of power. Politically conservative activists may try to overlay an organization's agenda with stern ideological concepts of law enforcement and welfare policy. But such doctrinaire people do a disservice to community groups when they try to impose their more exotic politics. Community organizations develop their own positions, ones that tend to have little to do with that world of parties, highly visible intramural fights, and the ideological arguments we are accustomed to think of as "politics," with headlines and television stories.[1]

A social change philanthropist on the right might contribute funds to help educate citizens about the virtues of prayer in the schools or the dire consequences of abortion, just as one to the left of center might sponsor an educational campaign in support of the First Amendment or of pollution control. Social change philanthropy, compared to traditional philanthropy, is more directed to:

- Helping to redress grievances, partly to reduce the level of protest.

- Helping to empower citizens to become more active and effective in pursuit of an approved set of policies. The more progressive social-changers want such empowerment to help citizen-based organizations to become more autonomous, more democratic, and more stable.

- Creating an environment leading to appropriate changes in legislation.

- Increasing the flow of funds available for support of social change organizations.

A more explicit list was prepared in the late 1970s by the Bay Area Committee for Responsive Philanthropy. The committee defined social change activities as:

1. Working for a fairer distribution of income or wealth; or
2. Working for increased social or political empowerment of oppressed people, especially among racial minorities, women, sexual minorities, the elderly, the handicapped, youth, working class or poor people; or
3. Working to meet the immediate survival needs of oppressed people.

These goals can be accomplished by:

1. Creating institutional change to eliminate causes of oppression; or
2. Providing services which empower people by meeting needs society does not yet recognize as legitimate; or
3. Creating alternative institutions; or
4. Researching and monitoring institutional responsiveness.[2]

The nonprofit organization is the primary instrumentality by which philanthropists implement such policies. No intrinsic differences exist between right-wing, centrist, and progressive groups in terms of their chosen forms of activity; all use the same instrumentalities to collect funds for distribution and to receive such funds for their various purposes. Understanding the universe of philanthropic enterprises is a necessary first step toward understanding how the progressive social change network operates.

The Philanthropic Profession

The philanthropic individual is the sun around which the confusing array of nonprofit organizations revolves. Mapping the universe of nonprofits is a relatively recent activity, increasingly important as philanthropy became recognized as a profession and as the number of philanthropic organizations grew. The regularizing process was begun by leaders of the major foundations who formed the Council on Foundations in 1949 and then the Foundation Center in 1956. Both of these organizations concentrate their attention on relatively large private foundations.

Two decades later Independent Sector was formed to encourage the fullest possible development of philanthropy and voluntary action in the United States. It now describes itself as a nonprofit coalition with 650 member organizations. In addition a number of universities have established research centers and a number of publishing houses provide reference books for use by aspiring grantees.[3]

The philanthropic universe with which these organizations deal is bounded by the Internal Revenue Service's definitions of collective activities exempt from taxation. Its Master File provides the most definitive count available of the number of entities in the field. Independent Sector has analyzed 857,512 tax-exempt organizations listed in the Master File in 1983.[4]

Independent Sector concerns itself with (a) the 366,071 religious and charitable organizations filing reports under section 501(c)(3) of the Tax Code (of which about 30,000 are private foundations) and (b) the 131,250 organizations filing under section 501(c)(4) and (c) approximately 340,000 churches that do not have to file tax returns.

Section 501(c)(3) filers, including private foundations, are religious, educational, charitable, scientific, and literary organizations, and those testing for public safety, fostering certain national or international sports competitions, or working to prevent cruelty to children or animals. Includes private foundations.[5] Section 501(c)(4) filers are civic leagues, social welfare organizations, local associations of employees; these are organizations promoting community welfare, charitable, educational, or recreational activities.

We are primarily interested here in the approximately 90,000 section 501(c)(3) organizations to which contributions are deductible on individual tax returns and that, again in the words of the IRS, have been

granted tax-exempt status with the qualification that their activities had to be substantially related to the exempt purpose of the organization and had to serve public interests. A further stipulation was that net earnings could not flow to a private shareholder or individual, and there were restrictions also on activities to influence legislation. Finally these organizations could not participate in any political campaign on behalf of any candidate for political office.[6]

Understanding the laws concerning these nonprofit entities and admiring their number must not obscure the function of the philanthropic universe in providing a flow of funds to an array of grantees. Some of these section 501(c)(3) organizations merely receive funds from various sources and use them for designated operations. Some both receive funds and make grants to unrelated organizations and individuals. Figure 2.1 is a simplified flow chart to illustrate that process.

Figure 2.1
Money Flows in the Philanthropic System

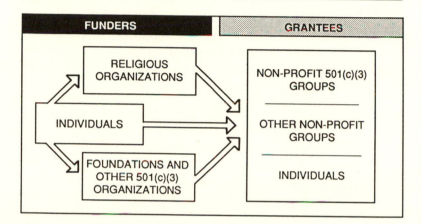

A much-needed, and far more sophisticated, framework to describe the bewildering array of existing section 501(c)(3) organizations was created over a five-year period in the early 1980s by Independent Sector's National Center for Charitable Statistics. Its Classification Task Force worked with the philanthropic community to create the National Taxonomy of Exempt Entities (NTEE). The taxonomy will be used in the coming years by major national organizations, including the Foundation Center and editors of *Giving USA,* to bring order out of the confusion of 501(c)(3) activities.

The NTEE's purpose "is to provide a system for classifying nongovernmental, nonbusiness tax-exempt organizations with a focus on philanthropic (IRS Section 501(c)(3)) organizations to accurately describe and define the voluntary nonprofit sector in the United States." Its categories for funding organizations, however, are less detailed than required for this book, although its categories will be helpful in our further discussion of social change grantees.[7]

I felt the need for a more detailed typology than currently shown in the NTEE in order to encompass the functions of the variety of funders and types of grantees that interact in the social change philanthropy network. The typology I developed is shown below:

Progressive Social Change Funders

Individuals

Churches and religious organizations

Section 501(c)(3) organizations:

> Public foundations, supported by many donors
>
> Private foundations:
>
>> Large, well endowed
>>
>> Smaller endowed (family) foundations
>>
>> Smaller nonendowed family foundations
>
> Corporate foundations
>
> Community foundations

Grantees (all of them 501(c)(3) corporations)

Intermediate, providing research and training on issues of national or regional significance

Intermediate, distributing funds to other grantees

Community-level activist organizations concerned with specific issues

Occasional forms of grantees:

> Service organizations, some in health or education
>
> Individuals

Although this list of actors in the philanthropic network may still appear simplistic, I have not found its like in any of the many books and articles I have encountered during this project, and I suspect that it may be helpful to others who are trying to unscramble the myriad of interconnections in the field.

A few publications give the names and addresses of a hundred or more of the better known funders, but many of the funders are small and prefer to operate anonymously for all but the IRS. Moreover, individual benefactions, the root source of most foundations, are largely untracked on their way directly to grantee organizations as well as indirectly to church funds and public foundations.[8] The population of grantees remains uncatalogued.

In the following section, however, I attempt to account for much of the money available from funders for progressive social change activities. Some fresh data are being published about the rivulet of funds flowing to and through church-related, corporate, and community foundations, all of which add to the more familiar information about the use of resources by the larger endowed private foundations.

The progressive public foundations are relatively new additions to the panoply of funders. They are generally without endowments but collect funds annually from a large enough number of relatively young and wealthy contributors to qualify under IRS rules that are less onerous than those for private foundations.[9] In form they resemble a prototypical public foundation such as the Audubon Society or the National Cancer Foundation supported by thousands or millions of small contributions. Examples of progressive public foundations in this study are the Youth Project, the Haymarket Public Foundation, the Vanguard Public Foundation, A Territory Resource in Seattle, and the Tides Foundation.

Also uncharted in the literature are the contributions that individuals and foundations make to what I have called intermediate private and public foundations. Sometimes these contributions are placed in a "donor-advised fund," whereby the intermediate organization, while not legally bound to do so under IRS rules, respects the preferences of the donor concerning further distribution of the money.

The Professional Work of Progressive Social Change Philanthropists

Profile of a social change philanthropist

The networks and tax-exempt corporations that collectively constitute the field of progressive social change activities in America are operated by serious-minded people, and it seems appropriate here to balance a discussion of abstract goals, forms of organization, and dollar amounts with some comments on those who have chosen to devote their energies to such work.

I do not use the term *professional* lightly. Social activists generally profess similar (and fundamental) ethical and moral precepts and agree on the importance of democratic consent and participation. More to the point, they generally fit the dictionary definition of one who makes a business of what an amateur might do for recreation or amusement. While some are certainly amateurs in the best sense of the word, others are devoting their lives and making their livelihoods in the field.

The field of progressive social change uses the skills of many specialists, just as the fields of health, city planning, foreign relations, and ecology (to name a few) are meeting grounds for specialized administrators, lawyers, financiers, engineers, and social and natural scientists. Many social change activists—funders, board members, and full-time staffers of progressive social change organizations—are drawn from the learned and applied professions, such as social work, business, engineering, law, and medicine.

Demographically, the field of funders is dominated by educated whites, with minorities well represented on foundation staffs and even more prevalent on the staffs of grantee organizations. At the time of this writing, the Council on Foundations has instituted a search for philanthropists who are members of minority groups. While no census has ever tried to enumerate the number and characteristics of social change activists, Part Two of this book covers much of what is known about the funding community as revealed in academic surveys of representative samples and in directories of known funders.

For most of the heavily endowed foundations, programs that would qualify under the rubric of progressive social change are only incidental to the larger purposes of the organization. A number of these major sources of philanthropic support, as well as some corporate and community foundations, assign highly trained and well-paid staff members to design and later administer progressive grant programs. Similar levels of expertise and remuneration can be found among staffs of well-established but unendowed public foundations (such as the Youth Project and the Tides Foundation) and among some of the smaller endowed family foundations. An executive position in a fund-raising community-based organization often leads to a position on the other side of the fence with a grantmaker, and work at a foundation may lead to a fund-raising or managerial position with a grantee. Equally skilled are hundreds of wealthy funders serving without pay as board members of foundations and often as regular staff.

An expression that has found favor in the field is that its participants are "investing in social change." Investing is serious business. Investing in socially responsible businesses is one form of endeavor, as further discussed in the next section. The term is also used, somewhat bitterly, by the staffs of many small foundations and activist organizations who see themselves investing their lives for the cause but remaining underpaid and lacking either fringe benefits or job security. Chapter 9 has some thoughts on this and other problems affecting personnel and the survival of small organizations.

But there remains the more generic meaning of investment by the confraternity of social-changers. In the world of commerce and industry, the return on investment is measured in dollars. In the world of socially responsible investing, the return is a mixture of cash, income forgone, and psychic income for being generous and civic minded. Social change funders have only psychic income for their pains, but they have invested their time and money just as systematically and professionally as any of the more traditional types of investors. They too have searched the land for opportunities to provide grant funds and sent out researchers to make site visits as part of the granting process. My further comments on this process of investment in social change are found primarily in chapters 6 and 8. At this point it is sufficient to note that strenuous efforts are made to maximize the impact of investments of time and money and minimize the inherent risks by channeling grants to promising organizations staffed with competent individuals who are able, within a reasonable time, to garner widespread support from other sources in their community.

There was a time when the major stock exchanges were beating the drums to induce small investors to buy common stock in American corporations. We still need such small investors, although the growth of pension trusts and other large agglomerations of capital tend to put the small investor at a disadvantage. The Reagan administration's attempt to provide tax benefits so that wealthy corporations and individuals would

make new investments in American industries was not successful, but the nation still needs such investment and, even
more, investment in human resources and an educated labor
force. By the same token, the leaders of the field of progressive
social change philanthropy have come to realize that they need
to attract additional funders, large and small, willing to invest
in programs to empower the disadvantaged, broaden the voter
lists, and increase the world's chances for survival and also willing to provide acceptable working conditions for those entering
the social change profession.

The role of socially responsible investing

Socially responsible investing is a related but basically separate
field from social change philanthropy. It is inhabited, however,
by the same or kindred souls. The field is composed of two
areas, the first representing concerns about the practices of U.S.
corporations at home and abroad with respect to environmental
pollution, production of military goods, and support of invidious
social policies (such as apartheid in South Africa). The second,
includes attempts to direct investment into more socially productive channels.

We do not need to dwell here on the first type, except to note
that a number of progressive social change philanthropists have
funded research and advocacy groups over the years. Examples
are the Data Center in Oakland, California, which compiles dos-
siers on the activities of individual corporations, and the Interfaith Center on Corporate Responsibility in New York City. Lists
of socially responsible investment advisors and the corporate
securities, mutual funds, and banks of deposit they favor are
widely available.[10]

Direct investment is the second and more relevant type, and
the U.S. Catholic Conference's Campaign for Human Development (CHD), for example, has devoted some of its resources
to projects that are typical of the genre: low-income housing
projects and worker-owned or cooperative business ventures.
The comments of Robert Zevin, vice-president of the United
States Trust Company in Boston and one of the leaders of the
entire field of socially responsible investing as it arose as a re-

sponse to the social protests of the 1960s, sum up some of the lessons learned over several decades:

> However, clean investing [in publicly traded securities] has two weaknesses as a social strategy. First, clean investing is an extremely weak way to exert effective pressure on the offending corporation. . . . [Second], both the acceptable and the unacceptable businesses may be doing the best they can to maximize profits under their respective conditions. In that case socially clean investing may distract attention from the real villain, which is a system that places too much emphasis on private profit and too little weight on public welfare.
>
> Alternative investing solves these two problems of clean investing. . . . However, the price of the increased social force of alternative investing is often lessened investment merit. Unfortunately, political films and newspapers are usually not as profitable as the *Wall Street Journal*; low-income housing co-ops do not provide the same financial possibilities as luxury condominiums. The investor anxious to do good with his or her money must often deliberately agree to do less well. . . .
>
> As a general rule, alternative investing is not for the meek or the modestly wealthy. For legal reasons, the minimum investment in a single venture is often between $10,000 and $100,000. For common sense reasons you would want to own a large number of these things if you owned any, since the risk in each individual investment is high. One way to cushion the risk of alternative investments is to structure them in a way that provides maximum tax benefits to the investor. But to benefit from those provisions you must be in a maximum tax bracket.[11]

A widely acclaimed example of the attempt to provide diversification for the smaller socially responsible individual interested in direct or "program-related" investments is the Institute for Community Economics in Greenfield, Massachusetts, which pools investments in land-holding trusts for low- and moderate-income housing across the nation.[12] A meeting ground for entrepreneurs in small socially responsible companies is being provided by the new Social Venture Network.[13]

At a more fundamental level, one of the stated aims of the professionals at work in the progressive social change community is to help generate pressure from grass-roots America for changes in social and economic policy; such changes as restoration of governmental housing programs would minimize the need for below-market investments by wealthy individuals. Many of the vignettes of grants presented in the Appendix fit into such a pattern to the extent they are empowering local groups to benefit more directly from the productive work of their membership.

The Flow of Philanthropic Dollars

Dimensions of the Funding Community

While the foundation community is engaged in studying the philanthropic system in order to serve the needs of both funders and grantseekers, the ultimate purpose of the philanthropic universe is to disburse funds for use by a variety of grantees. Finding where the money goes, as well as where it comes from, is part of the game. To date, the major sources of information about philanthropy have paid little attention to the social change network, which is in fact a miniscule sector of the philanthropic scene. So this section is devoted to a brave, perhaps foolhardy, and possibly first attempt to estimate the total amount of funds employed by the social change network.

Independent Sector's view

I begin with the broadest possible accounting of the monies collected and disbursed annually for philanthropic purposes and then whittle it down to suggest the portion directed to progressive social change. The broad view is provided by Independent Sector, whose most recent estimate is outlined in Table 3.1. The government sector primarily represents payments to private service institutions such as hospitals and universities.

Table 3.1
Independent Sector Revenues, 1984

Sources of funds	$billions		Percent
Private sector		$185.3	73.1
Contributions	68.3		26.9
Dues, Fees, and charges	95.7		37.8
Other receipts	21.3		8.4
Endowment (investment income)	14.0		5.5
Other	7.2		2.8
Government sector		68.2	26.9
Total		$253.5	100.0

Source: Virginia A. Hodgkinson and Murray S. Weitzman, *Dimensions of the Independent Sector: A Statistical Profile,* 2d ed. (Washington, D.C.: Independent Sector, 1986), 32, 117.

These funds included contributions by individuals and revenues to churches, and they supported most of the nation's charitable activities. The $253 billion figure represented not quite 7 percent of the gross national product for 1984, not a large amount given the range of socially useful activities supported in the absence of health and other national programs long established in other countries. As further detailed later, church revenues are of increasing interest to Independent Sector and amounted to approximately $50 billion in 1988. Many private foundations restrict their gifts to recipients of a given religious persuasion, but, at the same time, many church groups support one or more progressive social change organizations.[1] I take a particularly close look at the United States Catholic Conference's Campaign for Human Development in later chapters.

Funds through the 501(c)(3) organizations

The IRS reports that there are about 89,000 nonprofit charitable organizations filing under section 501(c)(3). Its analysis of the data showed that three categories dominated the scene: hospitals, educational institutions (including their pension funds), and publicly supported charities (including organizations, such as United Way, the American Cancer Society and the Red Cross, that supported those charities). Altogether, these three groups held more than 96 percent of both revenues and assets for this type of organization. Their program revenues include medical benefits and Medicare/Medicaid payments, academic research grants, tuitions, museum admission fees, and a myriad of other service charges made by these mainstream institutions.

Among the minor members of this group of tax-exempt organizations under section 501(c)(3) are all the other groups with religious, educational, scientific, health-related, or literary purposes or that are involved in testing for public safety. Hidden in these statistics are the revenues to a small number of social change philanthropies organized as public charities rather than as private foundations, as well as the funds for almost all of the community-based and research/educational organizations that receive direct grants from social change funders.

Focus on the private foundations

Probably no more than a third of the 501(c)(3) organizations are involved in grant-making of interest to this study, since most of the money from 501(c)(3) organizations goes to the support of hospitals and educational institutions that are not funders. The latest funding estimates of private foundations that are of interest to this study are for 1986 as compiled by the Foundation Center from IRS tapes and cover 24,712 nonoperating grant-making private foundations, 677 private foundations operating their own programs, and 250 community funds (32 of which were classified by IRS as private foundations). Table 3.2 shows the distribution of these 25,639 grant-making foundations by size of assets and total dollar amounts granted.

About half of the income of the listed 24,712 private nonoperating foundations was paid out in the form of grants; the remainder was added to assets or expended on overhead.[2] They spent about $6 billion for their philanthropic purposes, most of which was disbursed in the form of grants to other tax-exempt organizations.

As Table 3.2 shows, almost one-half of all grants emanated from the 1 percent of the foundations (277 in number) with $50 million or more in assets. And as the IRS report covering 1983

Table 3.2
Analysis of Private Foundations

Asset Category	No. of Foundations	Total Grants ($ millions)	Percentage
$100 million +	148	$2,456	40.8
$50-99.9 million	129	458	7.6
$10-49.9 million	846	1,151	19.1
$5-9.9 million	815	440	7.3
$1-4.9 million	3,739	744	12.3
$500-999,000	2,653	232	3.9
$250-499,000	3,065	167	2.8
$100-249,000	4,357	136	2.3
$50-99,999	2,733	69	1.1
$25-49,999	2,184	50	0.8
$10-24,999	1,947	37	0.6
Under $10,000	3,023	86	1.4
Total	25,639	$6,027	100.0

Source: Foundation Center, *National Data Book* (New York: Foundation Center, 1988); xii.

returns showed, the ten largest grant-making nonoperating foundations at that time (Ford, MacArthur, Robert Wood Johnson, Andrew W. Mellon, Rockefeller, W. K. Kellogg, Pew Memorial, Kresge, Lilly Endowment, and Hewlett) held total fair market assets of $12.6 billion, representing 17.4 percent of all the assets of all foundations, and gave out $1.1 billion or 26.2 percent of all grants by grant-making foundations.[3] These major foundations are obvious targets for legions of grantseekers and stables of proposal writers, and their potential for inducing explicit social changes is formidable although largely unexercised. Their historic role is lightly discussed in the next chapter, while here I discuss the generality of private foundations.

More on the large foundations

Independent Sector's pioneering studies of a broader set of the larger foundations include data on grants by category of recipient. Major shares of these grants go to such familiar purposes as medical and scientific research, health services, university facilities, research and scholarships, and religious institutions and functions. Comparable studies of the whole population of private foundations have not been made.

Independent Sector, in turn, relies upon data from the Council on Foundations' *Foundation Directory* for insights into the financial affairs of the set of approximately 4,000 foundations with more than $1 million in endowment or that make grants in excess of $100,000 a year.

The care and feeding of such large foundations is of primary importance to the Council on Foundations, and this is an appropriate point to discuss their study, *America's Wealthy and the Future of Foundations*, written under the aegis of the council, carried out at Yale, and published in 1988. The researchers at Yale based their conclusions on a quantity of historical and cross-sectional financial data and a detailed survey of a large sample of the foundations. They found that foundation assets were growing but were suffering from inflation and that, for a variety of reasons, the rate at which large foundations (over $100 million in assets) were being established had slowed, only six having been formed since the 1960s.[4]

The Yale study also discussed in welcome detail the many changes in tax law and personal preference that affect decisions concerning the establishment and operation of charitable foundations by wealthy persons of various religious, ethnic, and generational backgrounds. While one of the authors speculated that "big foundations may be a phenomenon of the Twentieth Century, treated in history books as the charitable byproducts of capitalist accumulation and dynasty formation," the overall finding was that the foundation world would continue to prosper even though the rate of formation of new foundations might slow.[5]

An Estimate of Progressive Social Change Funding

Distributing the $253 billion pot

Independent Sector's estimate of $253 billion for the nonprofit sector in 1984 represents the forest in which I hope to identify a few promising trees or the haystack in which I am looking for a needle. Independent Sector's estimate includes the cash contributed by individuals, the value ascribed to volunteers, and the revenues to churches, as well as revenues to all the grant-making foundations. I begin my search, sector by sector, for revenues available for progressive social change grantees in a typical recent year (for lack of precise data for any historical year or for the current year).

Independent Sector suggests that about 96 percent of the $253 billion pot goes for the direct support of service providers, largely in the health/human services and education fields. That leaves 4 percent, or about $10 billion, for all the other nonprofit organizations—scouting and peace activists, housing and antivivisection campaigns, environmental groups and the performing arts.

Only a small share of that $10 billion residual would be available for progressive organizing. Based on calculations in the rest of this chapter, the maximum amount of revenues directed to progressive social change activities might conceivably be in the range of $200–$300 million. That ball park figure represents 2–3 percent of the residual $10 billion.

Relevant grant-making by foundations

The estimate by the Foundation Center in Table 3.2 indicates that the group of 25,000 private grant-making foundations gave away about $6 billion in 1986. Unfortunately none of the estimators (the IRS, Independent Sector, and the Foundation Center) have detailed data on how the whole population of small as well as large foundations distributed these grants, but there is no reason to think that the whole group is any less conservative than the larger foundations surveyed.

A study by Professor J. C. Jenkins of 142 foundations known to support progressive causes found that even this group is reluctant to go beyond certain limits. He writes that their support "goes overwhelmingly to conventional charitable activities and established institutions. Social movement giving has always constituted less than one percent of total foundation giving."[6]

What share of the foundations' $6 billion might flow to the social change community, broadly defined, is anyone's guess. Based on Jenkins's findings, 1 percent would be a reasonably

optimistic figure, thus no more than about $50 million is con-
tributed by the foundation world to a wide array of worthy
causes—world peace and disarmament, environmental and conservation concerns, educational reform, civic education and
voter registration, and, among others, general community organizing.

To the monies from the private foundations should be added
the grants being made by the growing number of progressive
public foundations, many of them members of the Funding Exchange, and the smaller number of such grants that might be
expected from corporate and community foundations. Summary
data are not available, but a figure of $5 million might be rea-
sonable. Adding that amount to the private foundations' less
than $50 million still leaves about $50 million as a rough estimate
of the foundation world's total annual contribution to progressive social change causes.

A share from church-related funds

Until the Independent Sector's 1988 survey, no comprehensive
data were available on the participation of religious organizations in nonreligious eleemosynary activities. The survey of a
sample of the roughly 300,000 local churches in the nation was
conducted by the Gallup Organization and supplemented by
data from Giving USA. The data as finally adjusted indicates
that churches raised and spent about $50 billion in 1986, dis-
tributed as shown in Table 3.3.

The public and social benefit category appears to cover the
church-based contributions (including the Catholic Bishops'
Campaign for Human Development) that might be directed to
community betterment and progressive causes. Here again I
assume that the 1 percent rule applies, generating about $50
million from the $4.8 billion sum shown in Table 3.3.

Summing it up

Adding all this up suggests that about $100 million, compris-
ing about $50 million from foundations and another $50 million
from church-related activities, represents the full amount of

Table 3.3
Funding by Religious Organizations, 1988

	($ billions)
Education	$ 14.1
Human services	11.6
Health /hospitals	13.9
Public/social benefit	4.8
Arts and culture, International, and Environmental	6.4
Total	$ 50.8

Source: Independent Sector, "From Belief to Commitment," Summary Report, December 1988, 23. Data as adjusted by Giving USA.

grants available in a typical recent year for the support of progressive social change organizations.

Only a few grantees are able to live on such grants without being required to supplement them with other funding sources, such as individual membership dues and contributions, admission fees, sale of publications, and other charges. On the average, grants from foundations and religious organizations probably amount to no more than one-third to one-half of a grantee's total annual revenue. Thus the $100 million I estimated as the total contribution in the form of grants leads to an estimate in the order of $200–$300 million for total revenues for the operation of progressive social change organizations at the grassroots or community level.

This figure of $200–$300 million is equivalent to about one dollar per capita for the nation as a whole. It is about one thousandth of the $253 billion in revenue to the nonprofit sector of the economy. This estimate suffers from any number of definitional problems and from lack of accurate data, but a better estimate might not be much smaller nor larger, if all the definitional and data problems in this provisional estimate were cured or curable, and there is no strong evidence that the figure would be significantly larger or smaller in the ensuing years.

Social change grantees may also derive some indirect benefits from the mainstream charities, but the ability of the mainstream charities to absorb all the energies and monies available to them for their own functions should not be underestimated. Thus there is no basis for ascribing a dollar figure to the share of the $253 billion revenues that might have been sprinkled over social change grantees in the form of services or research reports that contributed to their work. The estimate of $200–$300 million will have to serve until better information comes along.

Part Two

A Portrait of Social Change Funders

4

The Emergence of the Progressive Social Change Network

Roots in Foundation Traditions

A bit of the history of social change funding, a look at philanthropy's religious underpinnings, and new thoughts about the philosophies of wealthy donors and their foundations are gathered in this and the next chapter.

Progressive social change philanthropy as practiced today is only another part of the history of social movements in the United States. Its taproots include Shays's Rebellion after the Revolution, democratic changes in the age of Jackson, the rise of public education, the struggle to emancipate the slaves, the outcry of the clergy and women's groups against the harsh doctrines of social Darwinism, the labor, populist, and settlement-house movements at the end of the nineteenth century, the factory acts and the women's suffrage campaign early in the twentieth century, and the coming of Franklin D. Roosevelt's New Deal.[1]

This chapter limns some of these linkages to our national history and may inspire some readers to delve further into past national debates, exploring the vast literature already in print. Adequate histories of the role of philanthropists in the progressive social change movements in America since the end of World

War II, however, have not yet been written. The historical sketches in this section are only a beginning.

The great foundations that were established at the end of the nineteenth century soon discovered that they could influence social policy by commissioning scientific research and educational programs. Their programs in the "social sciences"—economics, public administration, sociology, public education, and so on—necessarily involved critical judgments and recommendations for systemic change. John Simon, affirming the foundations' historic role in developing sound public policy after the congressional investigations of the late 1960s, quotes a 1960 article by law professor Albert M. Sacks:

The notion that philanthropy, to retain its character, must remain noncontroversial represents a fundamental misunderstanding of the institution which not only perverts its historical development, but also destroys its essential values. The most traditional of charitable purposes ordinarily require the acquisition, development, and dissemination of information and ideas, and they are not rendered the less charitable because such information or ideas are disputable and disputed.[2]

Prior to the Great Depression of the 1930s, the foundation world was smaller and relatively unorganized, each foundation following its own chosen path. F. Emerson Andrews, a long-term participant in the Russell Sage Foundation's public policy initiatives, singled out Edward A. Filene's Twentieth Century Fund for special commendation for its formulation of an effective public role for itself, as exemplified in these words from that fund's annual report:

The Fund believes that its research is not an end in itself but is justified to the degree it contributes to sound public policy; and that policies are useful to the degree that they result in action, which depends on widespread public knowledge.

In choosing subjects for investigation, the Fund has sought out, rather than avoided, controversial issues. It does this in the belief that controversy is often an index of the public importance of a subject and of the need for its impartial treatment.[3]

The foundations were besieged with appeals for "relief and palliative programs" during the depression, but Andrews notes

that by that time experienced foundation executives had ac-
cepted the doctrine that the "peculiarly free funds of foundations
. . . should be more adventuresomely expended for research, efforts to find cures, and prevention."[4] For thirty or forty years
thereafter, foundations became an endangered species, a point
to be remembered when reading critiques of their modest performance over the years. Congress in 1947 investigated foundations that owned profit-making businesses, drawing them into
the limelight for the first time. As sideshows to the McCarthy
era, hostile congressional committees, under Representative Cox
in 1951 followed by Representative Reese in 1954, held hearings
on the alleged ties between communists and foundations. These
hearings led to closer links between the foundations and to the
establishment of the Council on Foundations and the Foundation Center. Representative Patman's hearings, equally hostile,
began in 1964 as part of a general overhaul of the tax laws and
culminated in the definition of the "private foundation" and
all the regulations concerning them in the Tax Reform Act of
1969.[5]

From the perspective of a writer at the end of the 1980s, the
1960s can be seen as a time of embarrassments and a new self-
consciousness among foundations, with some of them awak-
ening to new opportunities and responsibilities concerning social
conditions and public policy, and others retreating behind the
untenable assumption that traditional grants in even such fields
as medical genetics would be forever beyond criticism. The 1969
act changed many aspects of foundation administration but not
the power of foundation boards to decide how and what to fund,
so long as special care was taken concerning grants affecting
electoral politics.

The foundation community produced a spate of introspective
books and committee reports as it accommodated itself to the
new age precipitated by the 1969 act, but I found literally no
discussions of progressive social change philanthropy (as analyzed in this book) in such incisive works as Andrew's 1973
Foundation Watcher or even in law professor John Simon's long
chapter on foundations and public controversy in the American
Assembly's 1973 anthology, *The Future of Foundations.*

That anthology, however, includes Jeffrey Hart's neoconser-

vative critique of *Fortune* magazine's statement that foundations
had developed into a powerful force for social change and human betterment and his denunciation of the Ford Foundation's
excursions into social activism during the 1960s with its grants
to the Congress on Racial Equality, black politicians in Cleve-
land, black educators in New York's Ocean Hill–Brownsville
district, the Center for Community Change, former members of
Robert F. Kennedy's staff, and several other minority organizing
projects.[6] Several articles in that same volume refer to the Peterson commission that was convened during the period just
prior to the 1969 act to consider the relation between foundations
and governmental agencies. Two of that commission's findings
are of interest here, first, that "a line cannot be drawn between
the fields of interest of foundations and those of government,"
but also that "only 0.3 per cent of grants were innovative."[7]

Nor is progressive social change philanthropy evoked in Waldemar Nielsen's treatments of the big foundations and the
golden donors, but he does commend the work of John Filer
and the Commission on Private Philanthropy and Public Needs,
established by the foundation community (using Rockefeller
Foundation money) to explore the implications of the 1969 act.
Filer brought donees into the deliberations for the first time, a
novel idea that was later institutionalized as the National Committee on Responsive Philanthropy under the guidance of Robert
Bothwell.[8]

Almost fifty years before Nielsen wrote *The Golden Donors* in
1985, the Carnegie Foundation had sponsored Gunnar Myrdal's
profound study of the position of blacks in America, *An American
Dilemma: The Negro Problem and Modern Democracy* (New York:
Harper, 1944). Carnegie's director, Frederick P. Keppel, was
"embarrassed" by the furor that followed publication of the
book. History may well record that the book's appearance was
a vitally important event in the development of the civil rights
movement that followed, but Nielsen observes that foundations
are still reluctant to delve deeply into controversial ideas about
society.[9]

Neilsen's main point is that by 1985 radical social ideas had
become the province of the "neoconservatives" represented by
Irving Kristol's journal *The Public Interest*, the "new populists"

represented by Richard Viguerie and the Moral Majority, and, in electoral politics, the ideologues clustered in the Reagan administration. No longer, wrote Nielsen, were the Fords, Rockefellers, and Carnegies the progenitors of ideas about government's responsibilities.[10] John Simon's affirmation ends with a call for full foundation participation in public affairs activities, with an emphasis on making policies effective. Nielsen ends his book with a prescription that the most important principle for a foundation to adopt is to have a socially responsible cause to pursue.[11]

Throughout the twentieth century, however, the large foundations have made vital contributions to the formation of many important social institutions and legislative initiatives, as well as to the growth of the foundation community itself. Many of them also made significant contributions to the social movements of the post–World War II epoch. Whether some of them will make comparable impacts in the future to improve the basic structure of American society is beyond the scope of this book, but their institutional memories can serve as sources of inspiration. For example, when the president of the Rockefeller Foundation, Peter C. Goldmark, announced the foundation's present (1989) intention to focus more of its attention and resources on "persistently poor Americans who have become the country's underclass," he quoted a 1913 statement by the foundation's first secretary, Jerome D. Greene: "Make sure when going into a community with a gift that the community has its own will . . . and its own resources, both material and spiritual to meet them."[12] Greene's statement came fifty years before the Carnegie Foundation's John Gardner's belated discovery in the 1960s about "how much could be accomplished by activist groups."[13]

Goldmark talked further of the need to create a new generation of researchers interested in this underclass and of the foundation's plan to help finance a multitude of community development corporations. He may also find that the kind of grass-roots community organizing long supported by progressive social change philanthropists is an almost essential precondition to the creation of the kind of community resources his predecessor, Jerome Greene, had described.

The Growth of Activism

Social issues faced in the 1930s and after

Chroniclers of progressive social change movements often ascribe their beginnings to the 1960s, but most of the basic components were in place long before that time. A few vignettes are sufficient to illustrate how social activism became part of the fabric of contemporary American society.

The first great institutionalization of the civil rights movement, for example, was the establishment by Roger Baldwin of the American Civil Liberties Union (ACLU) in the 1920s as a response to the incursions by U.S. Attorney General Palmer whose harassment of supposed subversions was a precurser of Senator McCarthy's reign of terror in the late 1940s and early 1950s. Also in the 1920s what may be the first of the social change philanthropic foundations was established, this one begun by Charles Garland, a wealthy young man dedicated to "simple justice" for blacks in America.[14]

The ACLU's skills were added to those of the leading black organizations, notably the National Association for the Advancement of Colored People (NAACP), to produce the civil rights movements of the post–World War II era. Segregation in the armed forces, in government-assisted housing, and in the public schools was acceptable policy in the Roosevelt years. Achieving desegregation and voting rights for blacks became important elements in the progressive agenda after World War II, with the 1954 decision in *Brown v. Board of Education* a milestone on the road to freedom.

While the environmental movement took its present form in the 1950s as a result of the fear of strontium 90 fallout from atomic bomb tests and after writers such as Rachel Carson had agitated about the degradation of our ecosystem from the widening use of chemical pesticides, the New Deal can be credited with the first systematic attempt to inventory and protect the nation's natural resources. The New Deal's record in reforestation and in fighting dust bowls and flooding is relatively familiar, but the work of the National Resources Planning Board in analyzing natural regions and river basins should not be forgotten.

Unfortunately, as John Friedmann and Clyde Weaver wrote in *Territory and Function,* the idealism of the early regionalists gave way to the more traditional practices of the Tennessee Valley Authority and other authorities. They made special reference to Benton MacKaye, the chief planner of the Tennessee Valley Authority in its early days and the primary force in creating the Appalachian Trail. MacKaye had contemplated a kind of regional planning and development that would use a region's natural resources for the benefit of the local population. Instead, the universal business class of which Heilbroner writes was successful in diverting most of the benefits of the TVA into corporate rather than community channels.[15]

Nevertheless, in at least four significant aspects of economic life, I feel that New Deal policies can be credited with laying the foundations for contemporary social change movements.

- For the first time, the federal government began to take responsibility for the stability and growth of the whole national economy and the equitable distribution of the national product. This responsibility was partly fulfilled by the social security and agricultural support programs of the 1930s and finally institutionalized by the Full Employment Act of 1947 and the establishment of the President's Council of Economic Advisors.

- For the first time, the federal government began to take responsibility to make housing and housing finance available to all citizens. The savings and loan banking system was overhauled for the home buyer's benefit. The memory of the principles that were the foundation of that system is the basis for contemporary protests at the methods by which the federal authorities are attempting to rescue the thrift industry. The public housing, middle- and low-income housing finance, and urban redevelopment and renewal programs that were vital features of federal policy beginning with the New Deal and continuing through the 1960s have been in decline since President Nixon's moratorium of 1973, but housing for all Americans, including the homeless, continues as a major issue.

- The New Deal also exhibited the government's feelings of responsibility for improving the structure and operating characteristics of the business world. It established the first effective regulations of the securities markets, although disclosures in the 1980s concerning massive violations of both the spirit and the laws in the stock and commodity markets suggest the need for even tighter regulations. In addition many New Dealers, such as Adolf Berle, worried about the concentration of economic power in large corporations and financial institutions with overlapping boards of directors; the Temporary National Economic Committee of the Congress, headed by Harry S. Truman, conducted extensive hearings that presaged current concerns about corporate responsibility and responsiveness to social issues.

• Unions were given an exemption from antitrust laws and, for the first time, empowered to organize major industries. The various unions more or less affiliated with the new Congress of Industrial Organizations and the older American Federation of Labor entered into a period of turmoil and occasional pitched battles, far different from the highly legalistic battles fought in the 1980s as the Reagan administration sought to reduce even further the waning power of the union movement.

Almost all of the present array of progressive social change grantees were established long after the New Deal had come and gone. One of the earliest examples of the genre, still favored by progressive philanthropists, is the Highlander Center, then known as the Highlander Folk School. Its efforts in the mid–1930s to train union organizers in the mid-South soon came to the attention of a few small foundations, such as the Schwartzhaupt Foundation, the Julius Rosenwald Foundation and, in the early 1960s, the Field Foundation. Funding in 1953 by the Schwartzhaupt Foundation of some of Highlander's work may be said to have opened the current chapter in progressive social change philanthropy.[16]

Early growth of the social change network

Thus by the early 1960s the stage was set for the emergence of a network of progressive social change philanthropies, despite the bruises left by McCarthyism. The 1950s had been the high point of the United States' world hegemony, although the Soviets got the bomb and the Cold War was well underway. Hardly anyone objected when President Eisenhower sent the marines into Lebanon and opted to replace the French in Vietnam after the battles at Dien Bien Phu. The American economy had expanded with vigor after worries about a post–World War II recession had faded; the recession of 1957 was seen as a mere blip on the screen, and Eisenhower's major economic concern as he left office was the emerging military-industrial complex.

However, Michael Harrington's *The Other America* appeared in 1962 and symbolized the arrival of the social concerns of the 1960s.[17] Following Kennedy's assassination in 1963, President Johnson was able to get Congress to pass the Civil Rights Act of 1964 and the first of his Great Society programs. The Office of Economic Opportunity recruited a number of progressive activists, some of whom were connected soon after with the Citizens Crusade Against Poverty, others with such dynamic organizations in the South as the Child Development Group in Mississippi, which used the Head Start Program as an organizing tool. The scene was later described by the Youth Project in the following words:

The most important influence on the development of organizing today [1984] was the impetus of the social and economic justice movements of the 1960s. During this period of unprecedented economic growth and prosperity, the Civil Rights Movement, the Student Movement, and the Women's Movement used mass demonstration techniques to call attention to the continuing poverty in our cities and rural areas, to glaring social injustices like racial segregation and discrimination against women, and to the social and economic cost of the Vietnam War. At the same time, the Federal Government's War on Poverty attacked the problems of poor communities through local community action and economic development. Together, these efforts won many tangible victories, including an end to legalized racial discrimination and the implementation of a wide range of programs to assist the poor. Perhaps most important, they appealed to the conscience of the nation, to the American belief in justice and equality for all, and thus encouraged many citizens to become active in working for social and economic change.[18]

The Youth Project authors go on to describe the "literally thousands" of grass-roots citizen organizations that were created across the country during a period of inner city riots following the assassination of Martin Luther King, demonstrations against the Vietnam War, and an increasing sense of economic insecurity as the war-induced inflation took hold.

While organizers such as Saul Alinsky were working in the Chicago slums and the organizers of peace marches found themselves mired in rivalries among the various causes, a few foundation executives began to make grants to organizations that could provide well-researched policies and a better sense of organizational strategy to some of the movements. Jenkins explained this process as follows:

It was as if virtually every conceivable social cause became the center of intense political concern. This tumultuous period served as a critical stimulus for foundations by identifying new social problems, creating an impending sense of crisis and generating a host of new political advocacy organizations that bid for foundation support. . . . Social movements themselves frequently fail to bring about the social changes they intend, but the political pressures they set off may well force through reforms anyway. The foundations do not initiate the reforms, but their funding determines which movement concerns and actors become permanent fixtures.[19]

Thus a network of progressive social change philanthropists emerged out of the confusion of the times. David Hunter of the Stern Fund, David Ramage of the New World Foundation, and later the staff of the Youth Project and Leslie Dunbar of the Field Foundation are leading examples of this process. Their role was to suggest from time to time to a variety of individuals and foundations that it would be desirable to focus funding on a selected list of issues and organizations. Their function in making their donors enthusiastic about nontraditional funding for social causes may be compared to the attorneys and personal advisors associated with the large foundations surveyed for the Yale study. Traditional advisors tended to accept the views of their donors and took responsibility for channeling the foundation's income into "a concrete series of contributions."[20] The Hunters and Ramages, however, advocated new views to the donors and helped create appropriate recipients for the grants.

The DJB Foundation was part of the informal network that operated during this period, and its operations were exemplary.

The foundation had been established in 1948 by Daniel J. Bernstein who died in 1970, his widow and three friends becoming trustees thereafter. Their final report covered their distribution of almost all the assets of the foundation to some 400 different organizations scattered across the country and involved in a broad spectrum of issues in the 1971–1974 period. The introduction to that final report, excerpts of which follow, is considered by many to be the finest available statement on the kinds of policies that began to characterize the progressive social change philanthropists who emerged out of the turmoil of the 1960s:

When [Daniel J. Bernstein] died in 1970, he had made a great deal of money, almost six million dollars of which came to the Foundation. By that time he had concluded that the chief enemy of mankind was not famine, flood, or disease, but quite directly the injustice of governments in general and of the United States government in particular. . . . The directions the Foundation has taken in the last four years have focused on the unkindness of man-in-power toward man-without-power. Through its history the DJB Foundation has turned more and more away from usual objects of philanthropic attention toward the victims of what seem to us increasingly to be official malevolence and indifference. . . .

National policies included systematic harassment of critics; stinginess to the poor; just enough attention to the middle class to keep them quiet; largess to the rich. Particularly reprehensible was the dropping of public programs, both Federal and state, that were often crucial to people's existence. Foundations were expected to pick up the responsibility that the government had dropped. Foundations on the whole responded. But they could not substitute for a humane government, nor should they.

The present Directors became absorbed in the question of what could be done with tax-exempt funds to protect against, expose, or overcome this official attitude. Inhumanity prevails when fundamental needs of Americans for shelter, food, medical care are neglected. Malevolence prevails in the deliberate persecution of unpopular or politically offensive individuals or minorities. Although neglect and persecution sometimes reflect majority opinion, this does not make them less evil. It does make protecting victims and educating the public more difficult and expensive. The DJB Foundation is not alone in its concern for these issues. Similarly inclined foundations and individuals are sparsely scattered around the country. Their advice and friendship have helped us during the past four years. . . .

The legal limitations on the uses of tax-exempt funds present continuing obstacles to reform-directed foundations and wealthy individuals. Mr. Bernstein took account of these obstacles early and chose a practical way of dealing with them. He spent money out of his pocket when foundation funds could not be used. Early in the 1960's he became convinced that the United States' role in Vietnam was in all ways odious, not least because it was shielded by official lies and stained throughout by cruelty and illegality. The rest of his life was largely given over to the attempt to change American policy about this shameful war. Virtually all of the small fortune he put into this campaign came from his own purse. Some educational measures could be paid for with foundation funds, but much of the activity he undertook could not. In this situation he learned the importance of spending tax-deductible and non-tax-deductible money side by side. The president of the Foundation, Mr. Bernstein's widow, has continued this practice of using private funds, both capital and income, to deal with needs for which foundation money cannot be used. . . .

In the report that follows, it can be seen in item after item that the problem we have tried to address is that of government vindictiveness or official neglect, sometimes both. We estimate that something more than three quarters of the assets of the DJB Foundation have gone into dealing with such matters. The delightful things that a foundation might offer in a benevolent nation—support of orchestras, choruses, ballets, string quartets in small cities and towns; additions to the stock of mobile and small libraries in the countryside; support of artists; public play areas, tennis courts, golf courses, swimming pools—have been made impossible for us because the basic needs that one might expect a decent government to supply are not met but rather exacerbated.

Foundation money is public money, temporarily at the discretion of semi-public trustees or directors. It can be seen as a small means of redressing the woeful maldistribution of U.S. wealth (especially when foundation money is supplemented by personal funds). . . . While private foundations cannot do much, they can do something to relieve frustration, restore dignity, and replace despair with hope.[21]

A detailed accounting of the actions and interactions of the individuals who constituted the network of progressive social change philanthropy in the last three decades may never be available. Few of the foundations have been as explicit in print about their feelings as the DJB trustees were, and none of the major participants, so far as I can tell, have written their memoirs. Forthcoming additions to our understanding of those times are an authorized history of the Field Foundation and a review of the Ford Foundation's activities in the urban field. In the meantime we must content ourselves with the less detailed and more synoptic research of sociologists such as Jenkins and others who have researched the post–1960s social movements and the contemporary role of funders.

My research for this book included interviews with a number of people who were actively engaged during those years at one level or another with some of the interesting players, foundations, and intermediaries. From that research I have constructed the crude chronological analysis that follows. The chronology should have intrinsic interest for anyone interested in the subject and may even help guide some future scholar to topics that should be covered more adequately and accurately in a full history of the network that emerged.

The network of moderately endowed donors funding progressive causes at the outset included the Stern Family Fund established in the 1930s, the Field Foundation (1940), the Taconic Foundation (1958), the New World Foundation (1959), and the Joyce Foundation (1948). By the early 1970s the list had expanded with new activism on the part of several older foundations and the establishment, by both the younger set of wealthy individuals as well as by older but equally committed people, of various funds and foundations, for instance, the Youth Project (1970), the Shalon Foundation (1969), the Abelard Foundation (1958), the Tides Foundation (1976), the Belden Fund (1970), the Needmor Fund (1956), several funds set up by members of such families as Mott, Ottinger, Norman, J. M. Kaplan, and Rockefeller, together with the Haymarket People's Fund and the Vanguard Public Foundation as the first of the regional public foundations in the field.

The Youth Project merits special attention in any review of progressive social change philanthropy. It was created by activists, such as Dick Boone and Lenny Conway, working with the Center for Community Change and other groups in the network to provide a means by which young people with inherited wealth could channel their donations collectively and effectively. It is almost unique in having field offices throughout the country working in tandem with its national office in Washington, D.C.

Its initial staff members and grantees have remained leaders in the field as executive directors of a score of organizations, for example: Drummond Pike with the Tides and Threshold Foundations, Dick Boone with the Field Foundation, Heather Booth with the Midwest Academy and the Citizens Action movement, Wade Rathke now a labor organizer, Steve Kest still with ACORN, Margery Tabankin at ARCA Foundation and now Barbra Streisand's foundation, Gary Delgado at the Center for Third World Organizing, Bill Mitchell of the Nuclear Safety Campaign, Si Kahn of Grassroots Organizing, and the late Willie Velasquez who founded the Southwest Voter Registration Project, Pablo Eisenberg of the National Center for Responsive Philanthropy, and Frank Sanchez still with the Youth Project. Lenny Conway, however, became an investment banker.

The Youth Project and the network of other funders worked closely with such existing policy research centers as the Institute for Policy Studies (founded in 1966) and the Center for Community Change and with coordinating organizations such as the ones that the DJB Foundation relied upon: the Regional Young Adult Program, the Southwestern Institute, and the Interreligious Foundation for Community Organization. Other organizations of this type were encouraged and funded over the years, such as the Midwest Academy, the Environmental Policy Institute, and the National Center for Responsive Philanthropy.

I know of no morphological study of the comings and goings of these individuals and organizations that played and play leading roles in the formulation of policy initiatives and the popularization of progressive causes. Some insight into their role is found in *Winning America*, with an analysis of each of the major causes that inspire progressive social-changers and an inventory of hundreds of individuals and organizations that could be relied upon for useful research and leadership.[22]

The mainline foundation world has its Council on Foundations, its Foundation Center, its Independent Sector, and a variety of other forms of mutual assistance for grantmakers. Less formal arrangements characterized the progressive social change community. The Youth Project in its own way served as a forum and information exchange in the early years for both funders and grantees and later brought many of the same actors together from time to time under the banner of the Progressive Constituency Network. A loose congeries of progressive funders met occasionally during the 1970s as ARF, standing for "associated rich folks," some of whom jointly and severally went on to form their own set of public and private foundations. ARF was eventually succeeded by the Council on National Priorities, now administered by the Funding Exchange, and another group emerged known as Doughnuts with the Threshold Foundation as its funding arm.

The National Network of Grantmakers, a progressive complement to associations of more traditional foundations, was created as a meeting ground by many of the same progressive funders in 1978. That same year the progressive public foundations created the Funding Exchange. Additions to the list of facilitating and communicating mechanisms in the 1980s include Common Practice, bringing progressive grantees together to discuss current trends, and, as one of a number of groups focused on women, the National Network of Women's Funds.

I found it impossible to diagram the network that I know exists either chronologically, cross-sectionally, or issue by issue. Documentation is lacking, the boundaries are indeterminate, the organizations form and reform over time, one issue is replaced by another as the year's privileged problem, and the key individuals move from job to job. The only really consistent attribute is the dedication of the individual donors and their chosen instrumentalities to the basic principles underlying progressive social change philanthropy and its concern for better national policies and the empowerment of low-income and minority people and their grass-roots organizations.

How Social Change Funders Think about Their Work

First Thoughts

One does not have to be rich to become involved in progressive social change philanthropy, nor does one have to stretch one's imagination to come up with any number of rationalizations for helping the poor to be able to help themselves. Our religious traditions can easily be interpreted to provide sufficient reasons, and other reasons can be found in our secular traditions. Although sometimes new immigrants and the working poor in nineteenth century America were spurned or subject to harsh discrimination, at other times assistance in getting reestablished in the community was generously offered, and, at least since the publication in 1933 of the report of President Hoover's Research Committee on Social Trends in the United States, the nation has been well aware of how inequitable has been the distribution of its income. Deep concern about the worsening gap between rich and poor, and the emergence in recent decades of what appears to be, for the first time in our history, a permanent underclass merely strengthen the moral imperatives of our culture to do something positive about these trends. As Independent Sector notes, "Not only can many diverse institutions trace their founding to religious institutions, but the values that motivate people to give and volunteer for the public good stem from religious teachings. Nearly half of total giving in the United States is to religious organizations."[1]

The ways in which moral imperatives are institutionalized in our culture are relatively clear and familiar. Less familiar are the psychometric studies that have explored the rationalizations of individuals who have internalized those imperatives and become active participants in progressive social change philanthropy.

The continuing challenge for the field is to turn ordinary philanthropists into people who will fund various avenues toward the empowerment of low-income and minority groups. How can the moral imperative be restored to the many people who have the means to share their substance with others but, instead, indulge in what has been described as materialistic and narcissistic life-styles? How does one convince the directors of a corporate charitable foundation to make grants that will do more than embellish the corporate image in its community? What further appeals, beyond those already being made by such groups as the National Committee for Responsible Philanthropy, inspire foundations to fund less traditional charities?[2]

Of course, not everyone accepts the dictates of the moral imperative or sees altruism as a virtue in the same way that Johnson does in his book, *The First Charity*. Johnson's view leads to a philanthropy devoted to strengthening a pluralistic grass-roots democracy, but there is a contrary view from the new breed of social Darwinists and their stable of conservative economists.[3]

President Derek Bok of Harvard University and Dr. William Sloane Coffin, Jr., president of Sane/Freeze, have their own insights into why not enough people are involved in public service—and, by extension, the funding of grass-roots organizing. Bok devoted his 1988 commencement address to his concerns that so many Harvard graduates were avoiding public service with its comparatively low salaries and prestige.[4] Coffin, long the chaplain at Yale, then minister at Riverside Church in New York, and currently president of SANE/Freeze, sees a nation with good causes to be fought for but with an educational system that fails to teach the ideals of service, as illustrated in these excerpts from Coffin's 1988 speech at an Outward Bound School banquet.

On the limits of charity:

As a pastor of an exceedingly mixed church in New York for the past ten years, where we have fierce feminists, lots of blacks, latinos, and gays and lesbians, I used to preach we all believe in harmony, but we also know that controversy is the life blood of our unity....

... the story of the Good Samaritan, it's helping people, generally one-on-one, and it's helping people without trying to change systems which caused them to need that help in the first place. It does not fool around with the structures of society. And as far as it goes, it's very good.... But it does not go far enough....

Let's ask, "Why are you at Outward Bound, and school administrators, and I and my colleagues in the churches so eager to serve charity and so loath to serve justice?" I think there are several reasons for this. ... Greed and power are far more hard-hearted than Dickens realized. And change comes much more in this world through struggle than it does from the belated decency of the rich.

Feed the hungry and you may be called a saint.... But if you question the reason for their poverty, you might be called a Marxist.... And that leads to the third question...why Outward Bound and the churches say they do not want to get political?

"We're not political," we say. What that really means is that we don't want to get into leftist politics. It won't hurt us to be called conservatives. So let's be a little more honest about this. The money tends to come from the conservative side. So "leftist" is what we want to avoid....

Today, and certainly in the years ahead, it is going to be more important to serve justice than it is to serve charity. And if we want to talk about social responsibility, we have to talk about an ability to respond to the needs of society as a whole. I would say that social justice is today, certainly in the third world, what civil liberties—freedom of speech, press and religion—was to America and Europe 150 to 200 years ago. It is an idea whose time has come. Social justice is not just a little wave on an inland sea. It's a sea tide oncoming.[5]

Coffin remarked that he did not see the kind of students he had worked with during eighteen years as chaplain at Yale working alongside him later as he campaigned for better housing in the slums, control of nuclear arms, or peace in Latin America. "Every country's education reflects that country's ideology," he said, noting that our students put their ideals in the closet after graduation and come to believe that the freedom to think is to be "vastly exalted over any obligation to do any good to anyone."

On the need for a different kind of education:

I am sure that Kurt Hahn [founder of the Outward Bound movement] would be appalled by what he would probably call a secular rejection of the moral imperative. . . . Hahn talked about "an aristocracy of service throughout the free world.". . . And I want to raise the question, "Is this service to justice, or to charity?" . . .

You have ambition. . . . It doesn't take you long to figure out that what our society teaches us to believe and what our society rewards as belief, are two different things. . . .

[Meanwhile the Rip Van Winkles of your present world] are either sleeping through or are having positive nightmares about a revolution called by Adlai Stevenson in the 1950s, "The Revolution of Rising Expectations." It is a revolution of human rights defined less in terms of civil liberties than in terms of social justice—the right to food, the right to minimal housing, the right to preventive medicine, and so forth. It is a revolution of social justice sweeping Central America, Latin America, many parts of Asia, and Africa. . . . What about First World countries like the United States? . . .

Now my suggestion [to Outward Bound students going back home to Watts, Harlem, or Detroit] is . . . get some community organizer out there to see what goes on, to be impressed by what you can do. . . . Let him help you translate this . . . because this isn't something you necessarily know that much about. But he does. There are community organizers in all these places, and they might be the ones, if you gave them a little time, to figure out just what it takes to serve humanity back home.

As for the rich, they need in their Outward Bound experience an experience of injustice that will make them want to serve justice when they get home. . . . Maybe they'll spend a lifetime thereafter combining a passion for the poor with a passion for the possible. . . . Outward Bound has a past to be proud of. But its greatest work lies ahead.

Neophyte social change philanthropists, regardless of whether their contribution is a few dollars, a thousand dollars, or volunteering with an activist organization, may feel like Outward Bound students at sea or on solo. They may be encouraged to learn (if they didn't already know) that their search for justice rather than charity has deep roots in the work of theologians and secular philosophers over the centuries.

The Religious Motif

Grants from a broad spectrum of church-based groups are often seen on the account books of activist progressive organizations, and the importance of such grants increases year by year. No survey seems to be available regarding church-based giving to progressive groups as a nationwide pheonomenon, and I have relied upon the notes and publications from the Catholic Bishops' Campaign for Human Development (CHD) for insights into the theological underpinnings of church-based progressive social change philanthropy.

In his introduction to *Daring to Seek Justice*, the Most Reverend James W. Malone provides an authoritative interpretation of the Catholic church's contemporary praxis:

The Second Vatican Council [1962–1965] concluded that the joys and hopes, the griefs and anxieties of all the people in the world, especially those who are poor, must be shared by those who call themselves Christian. . . . The Council acknowledged, however, that the church has no proper mission in the political, economic, or social order. The church is not a political party or a social agency: its essential role is spiritual. . . . but the demands of justice should be given high priority, because not only the effects but also the causes of social ills must be removed. And assistance should be given in such a way that the recipients would be freed from dependence on others and would become self-sufficient.[6]

Malone wrote that the Campaign for Human Development "is eloquent testimony that we have heeded some of the central imperatives of Vatican II. The Campaign's roots are in fact profoundly religious," and he described its four roots:

The first theme is the option for the poor. . . . The biblical standard sees a direct correlation between peoples' relationships with their neighbors and their relationships with God. . . .

A second religious theme flows from the first. The option for the poor is an option against what we today call "social sin,"—the unjust and oppressive structures that personal sins create and sustain. The person of Jesus comes forward to us today not only singly but in groups, classes and communities of people who are forced to live in conditions that impede them from experiencing full social participation and real human growth. These conditions often result from imbalances in political influence and economic power, and from discrimination based on racism and ethnic prejudice.

A third religious theme associated with the Campaign is self-determination. . . . Self-determination and active participation in the decisions that affect one's life are expressions of the fundamental religious belief about human dignity and self-respect. [in the words of Pope John Paul II]: "Do not say it is God's will that you remain poor. Organize for the defense of your rights and the realization of your goals."

A fourth religious theme is the need to promote a spirit of solidarity. The option for the poor is not a declaration of class warfare. The call to organize is also a call to involve others—literally everyone—in the campaign to secure a better world.[7]

Daring to Seek Justice goes on to document, almost day by day, the evolution and implementation of the idea of the Campaign for Human Development, beginning with the spur from Vatican II and the push from the riots of the 1960s before and after Martin Luther King's death, through a whole series of internal conferences and demands by such civil rights activists as James Forman of the Student Nonviolent Coordinating Committee. Many strong characters were involved in these discussions. The church responded in 1969 with appeals from the pulpits for funds, and the Campaign for Human Development was officially launched in October 1970. The 1971–1973 period is referred to as the time of setting directions, establishing criteria and procedures for making grants, and developing an approach to education: "These were years of tension, confusion, and controversy for the church, which was still adjusting to the post–Vatican II era, and the Campaign was not immune."[8]

Materials from the files of the Campaign for Human Development are sprinkled throughout this book, for it has become a vital part of progressive social change activities. CHD's funds come from a myriad of small donations during one Sunday a year in parishes throughout the country, but its funding processes are as sophisticated as any of those conducted by the wealthier individuals discussed in the next section.

Wealthy Individuals and Their Foundations

While much has been written about the big foundations, relatively little has been published about the current philanthropic proclivities of wealthy individuals except for the Yale, Boston College, and Vanguard studies upon which I have relied for this section. These three are relatively analytical, but anecdotal works, such as Aldrich's *Old Money: The Mythology of America's Upper Class*, novels such as those by Louis Auchincloss, and autobiographies, such as Adam Hochschild's *Half the Way Home: A Memoir of Father and Son*, can be read with profit.[9]

The Yale study on the future of foundations contains some interesting insights into the motivations of wealthy individuals in establishing foundations. Odendahl, writing about an elegant survey of a sample of such folk, says in her preface:

In this study, and in the field of non-profit research in general, causation cannot be established with certainty or precision. We deal here with matters of subjective intention on the part of hundreds of persons in a wide variety of community settings. . . . We can never know the "true" philanthropic motives of the wealthy, or the reasons for establishing foundations. . . . Although not conclusive, the purported motives help to throw light on a seriously neglected subject of study: charitable decision-making by persons of wealth. . . .

The popularization of foundations, as a result of Congressional hearings, media and public attacks, and rebellion of succeeding generations against the values of their parents, has had a negative impact on foundation creation.[10]

Overall, the Yale researchers confirmed that charitable giving as a percentage of income falls as income increases. The amount a wealthy person gives is based on a complex calculus involving financial analysis, prospects of death and taxes, nature of the wealth and its origins, and "age and gender and type of assets could be relevant."[11]

The survey of wealthy donors and their charitable attitudes was based on long interviews with a carefully selected set of 135 millionaires, including 79 men and 56 women (with a married couple equaling one respondent). Two-thirds were white and Protestant, one-third Jewish. One-third were "self-made," tending to be wealthier and older than the others. Forty-five of them were second-generation inheritors, 29 held third-generation wealth, and 10 held fourth-generation wealth.[12]

I read Odendahl's book for information about the interest of these wealthy respondents in progressive social change philanthropy but found little to report. The only substantive reference to progressive funding in the Yale study comes during discussion of a younger group of wealthy individuals who were reluctant to establish their own foundations: "The desire for personal involvement, especially on the part of younger wealthy people, has led to some rejection of the institutional aspects of formal grant making."[13] Absence of more detailed information about the activities of these younger wealthy people and the foundations with which they work, as covered by my research, is not restricted to the group at Yale; I found little understanding of social change philanthropy in my conversations with traditional funders and the staffs of national organizations in philanthropy.

The Yale researchers paid some attention to the tendency of the wealthy to restrict the amounts given to a specified share of their income, usually honoring the traditional concept that assets or capital should be preserved intact. This brought to mind a comment in the final DJB Foundation report that D. J. Bernstein recommended use of personal nondeductible gifts in tandem with his foundation's tax-exempt funds:

This use of non-deductible money as an adjunct to foundation-financed programs is not without precedent. But it is sufficiently rare to constitute an example which may be interesting chiefly to younger wealthy people. Much of the older generation of the rich seems to have been convinced by lawyers and money managers that the American Creed requires them to limit their giving to the use of tax-deductible funds, that principal is sacred, no matter how large a surfeit any one person has nor how urgent the needs of others. In regard to the DJB Foundation's assets, the Directors chose to ignore this conventional wisdom and instead to disburse capital as well as earnings. Our observation has been that preservation of capital becomes the main concern of too many foundations, causing them to worry more about investments than about programs. The Tax Reform Act of 1969 decrees a certain rate of giving by private foundations that sometimes means "going into capital." This sensible provision is aimed against hoarding of resources and non-income investments by foundations. It is a source of anguish for many foundations which are attracted more by the idea of perpetual life than by the opportunity to meet immediate and pressing needs.[14]

Much more revealing than the Yale study is the survey by Paul Schervish and Andrew Herman of Boston College, made with foundation support and published in 1988 as *The Study of Wealth and Philanthropy*.[15] The importance of their pioneering study for my book is the set of new insights it provides on why wealthy individuals become philanthropic, more particularly on why they contribute to socially progressive causes rather than who they are or, as covered in the Yale study, why they establish philanthropic foundations.

Schervish and Herman were able to conduct in-depth interviews with 130 wealthy or about-to-be-wealthy philanthropists across the country. About half of these acknowledged donors had made money on their own; half had inherited their wealth. The respondents were all white, two-thirds male, and mostly older than thirty and less than seventy years in age. They represented all shades of political opinion, but leaned to left of center, and a range of religious orientation spread fairly equally among Catholic, mainline Protestant, Jewish, or unattached, with a sprinkling of other or unknown preferences.

A brand new academic lexicon to describe the feelings of these people emerges in their analysis, including the terms and phrases *wealth and philanthropy in the sociology of money, biographies of the wealthy as dramatic narrative, liminality* (marking the transitions from early to later feelings about money), and *nomos patterns*, for the stages of individual self-development. What these wealthy folks, regardless of their different persuasions, ages, and backgrounds shared was the sense of freedom of choice and of being empowered in a number of important ways. They have the power to use time as they wish, including providing for a future "even beyond their mortality." They have power over the spaces in which they live and travel, and they can establish "bases of command":

A base of command is the array of positions and organizations through which an individual exercises effective control over the way other people act and think. Such power is rooted not just in the legally supported property rights associated with the ownership of businesses, financial investments, and real estate, or with the holding of executive positions, board memberships, and public offices. It derives equally from the non-legally binding exercise of authority whereby individuals exert influence by deciding to fund or not to fund certain causes, candidates or endeavors.[16]

They are also empowered psychologically, not only "feeling entitled and efficacious in regard to one's interests" but, as they learn the spiritual secret of money, "the scope of their self-interest gets increasingly broadened or deepened to include a greater diversity of people and needs."[17] Out of this empowerment comes a philanthropy that affords wealthy individuals

the means to move from simply being supporters to being creators or producers of philanthropic outcomes. . . . The substantially larger per-capita contributions of the wealthy, when purposefully leveraged toward accomplishing certain goals, can often single-handedly and directly spur the production of desired ends by, in effect, creating the organizational means needed to produce them. In sharp contrast to simply "matching" their concerns to pre-existing efforts, modifying existing institutions, or compromising with others over desired goals, philanthropy for the wealthy can be a way to further enrich their individuality and principality.[18]

Schervish and Herman identify some sixteen varieties of "social logic" among the wealthy.[19] Any one individual employs a mixture of philanthropic strategies or logics, some more pertinent to those with inherited money than to those with high positions in the business world, some as applicable to the non-wealthy as to the wealthy and to the secular as well as to the religious. My three-fold analysis of the Schervish-Herman "logics," retaining the original titles and adding a brief description, follows:

1. Seven of the logics give the donor a continuing sense of control and, as the authors suggest, may be most applicable to the self-made philanthropists:

    a. *Managerial* (philanthropy uses my organizational skills)

    b. *Investment* (philanthropy contributes to my business)

    c. *Productive* (my business firm is benefitting society)

    d. *Consumption* (my consumption helps others get services and education)

    e. *Derivative* (I give because I am a corporate official)

    f. *Noblesse oblige* (my capital is sacred, but I like to give part of my income)

    g. *Memorial* (I want to be remembered)

2. Seven of the logics describe what most funders, including progressive ones, might be expected to use:

    h. *Exchange* (I'll contribute to your cause if you contribute to mine)

    i. *Brokering* (I'm in a position to induce other wealthy folks to contribute to this cause)

    j. *Catalytic* (my contribution will help get others, rich and otherwise, to give)

    k. *Contributory* (I'm willing to give dollars but not time; I do not want to get involved)

    l. *Adoption* (I give by supporting a specific individual)

    m. *Entrepreneurial* (I make investments in small-scale entrepreneurial socially responsible ventures)

    n. *Programmatic* (I channel all my grants to one sort of grantee)

3. Two logics seem particularly descriptive of the psyches of both conservative and progressive social change philanthropists:

    o. *Missionary* (I use my grants to help transform society)

    p. *Therapeutic* (I work with other wealthy individuals on trying to understand the personal burdens of being rich, and we also work together on our giving programs)

Schervish and Herman provide a more detailed interpretation of this "therapeutic logic":

. . . when the wealthy, primarily those who inherited their money, move beyond the more limited responsibilities of the noblesse oblige logic by using philanthropy to reduce the privileged status accorded them by their inheritance. This approach is therapeutic because the inherited, in joining together to fund projects, also meet among themselves in workshops and retreats to resolve their dilemmas of personal empowerment. At the same time, they seek to extend this empowerment to the less privileged by tending to fund grass-roots organizations and by making decisions through democratic and participatory structures that include the recipients."[20]

Their comments apply directly to the relatively young and well-to-do members of the public foundations gathered together in the Funding Exchange and its Council on National Priorities, as well as to other organizations mentioned in this book, such as the Doughnuts and its Threshold Foundation and A Territory Resource. Many of these individuals were influenced by *Robin Hood Was Right*, produced in the 1970s by the Vanguard Foundation, one of the Funding Exchange's founders.[21] In that book, strong arguments are presented that young people with inherited wealth could do much better than contributing to their local symphony and attending charity balls by devoting both their money and their time to organizations that empower the disadvantaged. In addition to issuing a revised edition of that book and a number of useful directories for use in the progressive social change field, Funding Exchange is preparing an anthology of autobiographies of wealthy women who have become actively engaged in progressive social change philanthropy and in the affairs of its grantees.

Gaining Access to Social Change Funders

Progressive grantors and grantees are naturally symbiotic; each needs the other in order to function as social-changers, and each group needs to know more about itself and its symbiotic counterpart. The Schervish-Herman categorizations, especially of the missionary and therapeutic types, may help some grantors understand their own logics better and may help some grantees understand the motivations of potential donors to their organizations.

The committed social change philanthropists, conversely, need to know more about the grantees' world, and the next part of this book discusses some of the techniques that funders use to gain this knowledge, not the least of which is the personal site visit. But formal grant applications and site visits only come after contact is made between possible funder and prospective grantee, and the question, particularly for aspiring grantees, is how to build strong relationships with appropriate funders.

Naturally, given not only the fundamental symbiosis but the networking that characterizes the array of social change causes and campaigns, many of the funders and grantees already know each other. Some of the grantee organizations may have even been created by funder initiatives. More likely, however, the emergent grantee, having read one or more textbooks on fund-raising for grass-roots organizations or having attended a workshop on fund-raising as part of some funder's technical assistance program, begins drawing up a long list of potential donors as the first step in a fund-raising campaign.

The Grantseekers Guide, published by the National Network of Grantmakers, contains one of the best known lists of sources for funding grass-roots activists. In addition to a list of church resources for social and economic justice, the *Guide* has lengthy descriptions of a coterie of relatively well-known long-time funders, 80 of which offer grants across the nation and 92 of which restrict their grants to specified regions or localities. Most of the 111 funding sources listed in the Public Media Center's *Index of Progressive Funders* also appear in *The Grantseekers Guide*, the *Index* listing the grants actually made by the funding organization the *Guide* providing details on criteria and application procedures. Both have classified indexes so that a prospective applicant can identify funders' special interests.

The hundreds, perhaps thousands, of less well-identified grant-making foundations and individuals supporting America's innumerable worthy causes are not as well documented but constitute an essential part of any fund-raiser's working papers. I suspect that the universe of such funders is distributed by type in the same fashion as the results of my categorization of those funders listed in *The Grantseekers Guide*, as seen in Table 5.1.

Corporate foundations in the list are mostly large national or multinational corporations that tend to make grants only to organizations in the communities in which they operate. The usually unendowed public foundations include those mentioned elsewhere in this book: members of the Funding Exchange, the Youth Project, Tides Foundation, Threshold, Joint Foundation

Table 5.1
Distribution of Funding Sources in *The Grantseekers Guide*

	(Number of entries)	
Type	National sources	Regional/local sources
Corporate Foundations	13	2
Private Family Foundations and Individuals	52	52
Public Foundations	10	15
Community Foundations and Not Elsewhere Classified	5	23
	80	92

Support (JFS) and A Territory Resource, as well as a number of more focused funding organizations (such as the Ms. Foundation for Women and the Native Americans' Seventh Generation Fund). All of them conduct fund-raising themselves on an annual basis or hold donor-designated funds. Some of the community foundations are general-purpose facilities for their localities (such as the Boston Foundation/Permanent Charity Fund or the California Community Foundation), but some have been set up by professional associations or special-interest groups to raise and channel funds to selected causes.

In Table 5.1 I counted together the variety of private foundations and funds obviously established by particular individuals. Some are endowed, in the range of a few million dollars to the hundreds of millions for major foundations, such as Ford, Carnegie, and Mott. Some have endowments that are significantly smaller than the actual amounts of grants awarded in a given year from annual contributions by the founders.

"Must have experience in fund-raising from private foundations and individuals" is a phrase found in the job descriptions
circulated by social change organizations from time to time. The
ability to gain access to the appropriate source of wealth is the
stock-in-trade of the successful manager of a progressive think
tank or grass-roots organization, and the requisite knowledge
of how different wealthy families go about their philanthropic
business comes more from experience and gossip than from a
printed directory.

As an example, the *Guide*, not surprisingly, does not list the
doughty Rockefeller Foundation but does include the even more
doughty Rockefeller Brothers Fund and Rockefeller Family
Fund, but experienced fund-raisers know about an increasing
number of other sources established by younger members of
that family. Other known progressive funders include heirs of
many of America's great fortunes such as Mellon and Reynolds;
some are noted in passing in this book and are generally not
visible in the *Guide*'s list, but the array of Mott family philanthropies that does appear in the *Guide* provides a more detailed
example of such relationships within a family.

The Charles Stewart Mott Foundation tops the list of the various Mott family funds. Established in 1926 by a major stock-
holder in General Motors Corporation and with an endowment
currently valued about $500 million, it has a highly regarded
record in providing seed money to numerous organizations for
what it calls local "community self-improvement." It thus rated
being listed in the ranks of progressively oriented foundations,
along with Mott's widow's foundation (the Ruth Mott Fund,
granting about $1 million a year) and his daughter's philan-
thropic endeavors (the C. S. Fund/Maryanne Mott Charitable
Trust, granting about $1.5 million annually, not including dis-
tributions through her donor-advised funds: the Resource Fund
and the CR Fund at the Youth Project and the Ready Fund held
at the Tides Foundation).

Also listed are his son Stewart's array of organizations to
"carry out the administrative responsibilities for Mr. Mott's personal philanthropy," derived from his inheritances: the Stewart
R. Mott Trust, Stewart R. Mott and Associates, and Spectemur
Agenda. According to the *Guide*, Stewart was educated at MIT

and Columbia and after graduation in the early 1960s worked as a teacher, then as executive trainee in companies controlled by his father. He also worked as a volunteer speaker and fund-raiser for Planned Parenthood, to which he had donated more than $1 million.[22] As necessary background for grantseekers, the *Guide* describes the perhaps not so-unusual orgins of these organizations:

In 1965, he discussed with his father a broadening of the family foun-dation's interests to include population control, arms limitation, and other new programs. When it was decided that such a broadening was not consistent with the foundation's goals, Stewart Mott embarked on his own program of philanthropy. . . . Mr. Mott's primary interests are: (1) peace, arms control, and foreign policy; (2) family planning and population issues; and (3) government reform and political educa-tion. His preference is to support activist projects rather than research-oriented activities, and projects that are national in scope, not local or regional.

Stewart Mott is more public about his activities than many donors similarly situated, but the *Guide* makes it clear that he exercises his privilege of funding by his own wishes and in his own time; there is no formal application procedure, and no more than five new projects a year will be funded. Indeed, social change fund-raisers come to understand that each funding source has its own ways of doing business with an unknown applicant. Sometimes only invited applications are considered. Often telephone inquiries are discouraged. Some specify brief letters and specific dates for application, others want full-blown proposals to be considered at random times. Some have strict minimum and maximum grant amounts, and most have clear statements that rule out grants to capital construction programs, endowments, or individuals.

The portrait of progressive social change funders that emerges in this chapter is like a two-foot-long group photograph taken at a college or family reunion with hundreds of faces; one can tell little about the private actions and reactions of the people behind the faces. What they have in common is a serious con-tinuing interest in funding the social causes of their own choosing, as well as a wish that more people were present when the photograph was taken. Their collective experiences as funders in dealing with grantees and actually making grants are covered in more detail in the chapters that follow.

Part Three

A Portrait of Social Change Grantees

6

Definitions of a Social Change Grantee

The DJB Foundation's Model

Few things please a progressive funder more than finding and funding a suitable grantee, who may even be one of President George Bush's "thousand points of light." Funders have discovered that the job of identifying and evaluating potential grantees requires time, patience, good staff, lots of paperwork, and a round of site visits and telephone calls.

While funders begin with a feeling that there are many likely prospects, most minority groups at the lower end of the socio-economic spectrum need a great deal of encouragement and sometimes technical assistance to be willing to step forward and to be able to put together an acceptable proposal. The process gets no easier as the years go by, for funding guidelines change and a new group of grantees must be found to replace those who have had what a given funder deems to be their fair share of support.

As the number of funders interested in helping empower grass-roots organizations increases, so does the flow of applications for support. I have learned that many people know as little about the types of grantees as they profess to know about the progressive funding sector, and thus I have written this and the next chapter to show how funders approach the task of

putting money to work in the field. To illustrate the spirit guiding
the policies of secular progressive social change funders, I begin
with a few more excerpts from the final report of the DJB Foundation, whose sentiments are as inspirational now to those in
the progressive funding community as they were when for-
mulated in the early 1970s. These excerpts are followed by a
look at the criteria and guidelines currently in use by the Campaign for Human Development of the United States Catholic
Conference (USCC).

Here are some of the operating practices adopted by the directors of the DJB Foundation in January 1971 (and still considered by many as the best statement of socially relevant
principles) to guide them in defining and selecting grantees:

- We decided to concentrate on those groups and programs generally
  ignored by conventional foundations because they were "controversial." These turned out to be the poor; GI's, deserters, and draft
  refusers; black, yellow, and brown groups; convicts and ex-convicts—
  all those habitually neglected or picked on by authority. Examples
  are Chicago clinics and legal centers; GI's in Japan, Germany, and
  Indochina; prisoners' unions; defense of Indians' personal and property rights.

- We decided to operate on a nationwide scale, despite our modest
  resources, and to aim at encouraging those struggling for a foothold
  in many places. A small grant from an unknown foundation in West-
  chester County, we learned, did wonders for morale in Arkansas,
  Montana, New Mexico, or Mississippi. . . .

- We decided to give when small grants could make a difference. Our
  effort has been to help small groups get on their feet, but not to
  commit the Foundation to their lasting support. Thus we have by and
  large kept away from adding a few thousand dollars to large institutional budgets, no matter how worthy the undertaking, as we have
  kept away from general-support grants to churches, universities, and
  the like. . . .

- We agreed that money with strings is generally worse than no money
  at all. We often noticed that foundations, large ones mainly, made
  generous grants tied to demands for behavior, personnel changes,
  attitudes, or results that debased the project as conceived by its proponents. We have tried to gather information, make a fair judgment,
  and then make a grant without imposing our own ideas. . . .

- We believed that real change must come from the roots of American society. As middle-aged, liberal Americans we had seen enough history to realize that any change from the top was likely to be paternalistic or token, and seldom designed really to lead toward independence. So we have concentrated on aid to small groups organizing to help themselves and their neighbors and to resist the twin juggernauts of official and corporate power. DJB grants thus gravitated toward ghettoes and barrios in the city and toward neglected communities in rural areas.

These are the ideas that have guided us, and we are satisfied that they have served us well. We hope this report will be useful, particularly to those young people coming on the scene with money and with a desire to improve a confused and distressed society.[1]

DJB was in full swing as the Campaign for Human Development was getting itself organized and fighting its battles for acceptance within the Catholic Church. CHD's support of community organizing sounded to some parishioners as too agitational and provocational and certainly not what the church should get involved in. Nevertheless, CHD has become a permanent part of the scene, not only within the church but as a leader in the progressive funding community. Moreover, CHD's descriptions of the projects it funds are far more revealing than those in most foundation reports; they provide the grist for the following section. And CHD's guidelines, with minor exceptions, are fully representative of current practice.

Criteria of the Campaign for Human Development

The emergence of the Catholic Church's CHD strengthened and stimulated both secular and church-related ventures into the field of progressive social change philanthropy. The authors of *Daring to Seek Justice: People Working Together: The Story of the Campaign for Human Development: Its Roots, Its Programs and Its Challenges* write that CHD has had a positive impact on the church itself and has become the largest funder of its kind in the country.[2]

Daring goes into considerable detail about the internecine battles concerning CHD guidelines, which were ultimately drafted to assure that grantees did not violate the church's moral teachings, especially concerning abortion. Although other funders are clearly not bound by such restrictions, CHD's record has been widely praised by secular leaders, and *Daring*'s writers could not resist a few quotations to prove the point. A few examples follow.

Mr. George Pennick of the Mary Reynolds Babcock Foundation says that "CHD is exceptional in the way it is able to identify grassroots groups before anyone has even heard of them. There are numbers of groups that are now major factors because of CHD. . . . You would think that the larger an organization and the more broad-based its constituency, the more conservative it would be. But CHD is just the opposite—it takes chances."

Others in the funding community echo this praise of CHD's willingness to take chances. Mr. Louis Knowles of the Council on Foundations says that what is unique about CHD is that "it doesn't seem to be afraid to fund organizations that cause controversy in their communities—that's hard to find."

Heather Booth of the Midwest Academy, a training school for organizers, says "CHD has fostered less factionalism, less sectarianism, because of the diversity of groups that it funds. CHD is in fact building democracy."

And Ms. Lois Roisman of the recently established Jewish Fund for Justice believes that "CHD has made it 'all right' to fund in this area. You can always say, 'Well, the Catholic Church is funding that.' "[3]

CHD's willingness to fund community organizing is in line with current papal and episcopal social doctrine. Community organizing, however, stretches the limits of propriety for the more conservative members of the church, so that *Daring* takes pains to justify its emphasis on the practice in words that deserve attention outside the church.

Modern community organizing can trace its roots to the work begun by Mr. Saul Alinsky in the 1940s. Alinsky was often branded by liberals as well as conservatives with negative epitaphs such as "revolutionary" and "leftist." According to P. David Finks, author of a biography of Alinsky (*The Radical Vision of Saul Alinsky*), "his ideological mentors were not Marx and Lenin. . . . Alinsky considered himself a political descendent of a long line of American activists that included Patrick Henry, John Adams, Thomas Paine, Thomas Jefferson and James Madison." The famous French Catholic philosopher, Jacques Maritain, Alinsky's friend for twenty years, called him "a living, heroic witness of the Judeo-Christian tradition . . . a great soul, a man of profound moral purity and burning energy."

As Alinsky did with his predecessors such as the labor organizer John L. Lewis and nineteenth century populists, contemporary organizers freely change Alinsky's approach, style, tactics and strategies to suit the current scene. Bishop Friend said that Alinsky's methodology, "is not intrinsically good or bad; it is the use to which it is employed that is important." In any case, groups employing "Alinsky" methodology receive grants only if they meet CHD funding criteria and guidelines.[4]

How successfully CHD has followed its own rules can be seen in the sample of its projects that are included in the Appendix. The rules below are part of the formal preapplication instruction to be followed by applicants for CHD support.

A. Criteria
   1. The project must benefit a poverty group. . . .
   2. Members of the poverty group must have the dominant voice in the project. . . .
   3. Funding will not [ordinarily] be considered for projects which can be funded by monies available from the private or public sector. . . .
   4. No CHD funds will be granted to organizations that would utilize CHD money to fund other organizations.
   5. The project activity for which funding is requested must conform to the moral teachings of the Catholic Church.
B. Guidelines
   1. Projects which are innovative and demonstrate a change from traditional approaches to poverty by attacking the basic causes of poverty and by effecting institutional change. CHD defines institutional change as:
      a. Modification of existing laws and/or policies.
      b. Establishment of alternative structures and/or redistribution of decision-making powers.
      c. To a lesser extent: Provision of services which result in the achievement of (a) and/or (b); or leads the recipient community to focus on (a) and/or (b).
   2. Projects which directly benefit a relatively large number of people rather than a few individuals.

3. Projects which generate cooperation among and within diverse groups in the interest of a more integrated and mutually understanding society.

4. Projects which document that as a result of CHD funding there are possibilities of generating funds from other sources or of becoming self-supporting within the timelines established in the proposal.

C. Projects Not Meeting CHD Criteria and/or Guidelines

The following general classifications do not meet CHD criteria and/or guidelines:

1. Direct service projects (e.g., day-care centers, recreation programs, community centers, scholarships, subsidies, counseling programs, referral services, cultural enrichment programs, direct clinical services, emergency shelters and other services, refugee resettlement programs, etc.)

2. Projects controlled by government (federal, state, local), educational, or ecclesiastical bodies.

3. Research projects, surveys, planning and feasibility studies, etc.

4. Projects which have been operating for several years on funds from other funding agencies.

5. Projects sponsored by organizations which at present receive substantial sums from other funding agencies, unless the applicant documents that this project cannot be funded by these agencies.

6. Individually owned for-profit businesses.

With only a few exceptions and further interpretations, CHD's requirements might be used by most other social change funders, but undoubtedly a statement concerning moral teachings would be left out of application forms from secular funders. I have found that some grantees (CHD's and others') conclude that certain requirements (for example, a set limit on the number of years that fundings will be offered to any one project, the expectation that a grantee can become financially self-sufficient, or the prohibition against research) are unrealistic and even counterproductive. However, in the process of evaluating proposals, strategic exceptions are made to almost all of the stated requirements, including in the case of grass-roots worker-owned or cooperative businesses the stricture that for-profit enterprises will not be funded.

The portrait of the funders in Chapter 5 might resemble a

group photograph, but a collective portrait of the grantee population would be more like a newspaper photograph of a crowd
scene. No one has yet published a national or even a regional
directory of seasoned grantees; each funding organization must
compile its own topical list. The descriptions of individual grantees classified by type in the Appendix illustrate the variety of
organizations that have gained funders' favor in recent years.
However, my analyses of 1,482 grants in the next chapter constitutes a more statistical picture of the field.

7

A Typology of Social Change Grantees

Constructing a Typology

My analyses of the grants made by CHD and a number of other social change funders are the basis for some useful current generalizations about the range, scope, and form of grantees. CHD does a particularly fine job in coding each of its grantees in a number of different ways, but I modified CHD's categories to accommodate data from other funding sources to produce the typology used hereafter.

Progressive grantees can be categorized in many ways, reflecting subject matter, type of activity, and characteristics of the involved population. A primary distinction among them is the geographic scope of their interest. Practically all of them fit into one of the following two major categories.

1. Local and statewide community-based activist organizations.
2. Intermediaries, a term I use to describe grantees that offer public-policy or issues research to national decisionmakers and to grass-roots organizations across the country.

Grantees perform many functions in the communities they serve. Among the generic activities to be funded are basic organizing, researching issues and educating local citizens about them, and building up local communications media and cultural facilities. Funders also give grants for general support of the organization and for technical assistance and staff training, including funds to encourage travel and networking. Occasionally, they will ask a grantee to redistribute grant funds to designated organizations. Outside of the usual framework into which grantees fit are the organizations promoting socially responsible investing or receiving funds for housing and community development projects or for small business development and loan programs.

A working typology with eight broad subject areas describing the work of recent grantees emerged from my analysis of grants by CHD and five other funders.

1. General community organizing, including church-based activities
2. Economic justice, civil rights, women's issues, legal aid, and voter registration
3. Economic security, jobs, and economic development
4. Housing and community development, inner city problems, and tenants' rights
5. Environmental concerns, toxics, energy, and conservation
6. Children, youth and families, and health issues
7. Schools and public education
8. National security, peace, and arms control issues

Individual grantees can be further described (as CHD does in its reports) in terms of subject area, nature and form of their activities, geographic scope (national, statewide, or local, including urban/rural split), and racial and ethnic composition.

The fundamental difference between the kind of social change grantee considered here and most of the hundreds of thousands of tax exempt entities covered in Independent Sector's National Taxonomy resonates in CHD's criterion 2: "Members of the poverty group must have the dominant voice in the project." In the language of the social change community, this criterion means that any local or statewide organization is "owned" by its embattled members, not just operated for their benefit.[1]

The NTEE coding scheme does not refer to such ownership,

implying that most of the nonprofit entities it covers are created to provide services for—rather than by—the targetted benefici- aries, but it goes into considerable detail concerning the subject matters treated, the kinds of activity entailed, and the demo- graphic character of the major group served. The list of subject groups in the NTEE is all-encompassing, by design, but only one designation can be given to an individual grantee organi- zation.

Unfortunately, a large proportion of social change grantees span more than one field, for example, fitting simultaneously into such NTEE major group codes as consumer protection, em- ployment/jobs, and housing/shelter. I found it impossible to as- sign single NTEE activity/program codes to the run of multifaceted social change grantees and thus was impelled to develop the typology discussed in the next section.

Analysis of Recent Grants by Social Change Funders

Coding 1,482 recent grants from six major funders

Many books on the subject of progressive social change phi- lanthropy provide their readers with a few illustrative case stud- ies of grantees. Johnson in *The First Charity*, for instance, discusses three: BUILD (Baltimoreans United in Leadership De- velopment), MOP (Metropolitan Organizations for People, Den- ver), and UNO (United Neighborhood Organization of South East Chicago).

However, I had long wanted a broader understanding of the scope of funding in the field and saw no other way to view the distribution of grants among the eight subject areas of my ty- pology than by analyzing a representative sample of grants ac- tually made by leading funders. My computerized database soon contained 1,482 grants made over the past few years, aggregat- ing almost $26 million, as they appeared in annual reports of the following six foundations:

1. *Campaign for Human Development*, Washington, DC
       Funded Projects 1986
       Funded Projects 1987

2. *The Youth Project*, Washington, DC
   Annual Report 1986–1987
   Annual Report 1987–1988

3. *The Women's Foundation*, San Francisco, CA
   Annual Report 1987

4. *Joint Foundation Support*, New York, NY (administering some fifteen families' and individuals' philanthropic funds)
   Annual Report 1986–1987

5. *The Tides Foundation*, San Francisco, CA (conducting its own granting from contributed funds as well as administering a number of donor-advised funds)
   Annual Report 1987

6. *Threshold Foundation*, San Francisco, CA (in effect a donor-advised fund administered by, but not included, in the Tides Foundation report)
   Annual Report 1987

My sample of empirical data is not statistically pure. It is biased toward unendowed funding organizations that must secure annual contributions, but, except for CHD whose funds come from a once-a-year collection in parish churches, the individual donors tend to maintain a high level of contribution year after year (in the range of $1,000–$100,000). The sample is further biased toward CHD and the Youth Project, each represented by two years' worth of grants. The other four funders have only one year's worth in the array. Among my sample's other deficiencies are the facts that grants made in these late years of the 1980s are different than might have been seen in earlier periods and may not be representative of granting patterns hereafter, and, lastly, that some grantees in the database have received grants from more than one of the funders and may have been funded in each of CHD's and the Youth Project's two cycles.

Nevertheless, I know of no other comparable cross-sectional analysis in print. I have had a long-standing interest in seeing the distribution of such grants by subject and race, among other dimensions, and thus a first step was to classify each grant as well as I could using the eight-fold code I had developed. The coding can also be challenged, for some of the descriptions in the foundations' annual reports were minimal, and some grants could have fitted into another category other than the one I assigned.

I found it necessary to recode each of the projects to place them into my eight-fold list, for the CHD encoders had placed into the social development category projects ranging from church-based and general community organizing/economic justice projects through tenant organizing and inner-city housing as well as jobs, worker rights, and education projects to projects dealing with health, family, prison reform, and toxics. Table 7.1 begins the resulting analysis.

Although the total amounts granted by CHD and the collection of other funders are more or less equivalent in amount, sharp differences appear. The average CHD grant is considerably larger than the average grant made by the other five funders. CHD, by its charter, does not fund organizations concerned with national security issues or organizations operating overseas, as the others do. The concentration of CHD grants for community organizing is notable, as are related grants for organizing around economic issues (category 3) and around housing and neighborhood issues. In contrast, the other funders are clearly more heavily invested in questions of economic justice, civil rights, environmental issues, and the issues affecting people and their health.

I was also interested in the geographic distribution of the grants in my sample (see Table 7.2). In the tabulation of grants by state, some of the figures are skewed by the concentration of policy-oriented, nationwide, groups in such centers as Washington, D.C., New York, and California, and by the practice of the Women's Foundation of keeping most of its grants within California. CHD's practice of allocating equal amounts of funds to its regional agglomerations of dioceses means that grants are widely dispersed among the states; only Maine did not receive CHD money in those years. CHD grants were notably more numerous in well-populated central and mid-Atlantic states (Illinois, Iowa, Michigan, New Jersey, Ohio, Pennsylvania, Wisconsin) than for the other five funders, some of whose preferences for groups in the upper south and smaller states such as Montana show through.

If and when better data become available in the future, inter-

Table 7.1
Distribution of 1,482 Grants by Subject

Short title of grant category	Number	Dollars granted By CHD ($000)	By others ($000)
1. General community organizing....	272	$ 4,655	$ 899
2. Economic justice..............	275	1,149	3,621
3. Economic security.............	216	3,682	983
4. Housing and community dev......	109	2,279	380
5. Environmental concerns.........	118	245	1,710
6. People and health.............	169	1,033	1,676
7. Schools and public education...	132	261	1,361
8. National security; peace.......	191	-0	1,952
Total	1482	$13,304	$12,602
		$25,906	

Table 7.2
Distribution of Grants by State

	CHD	Others		CHD	Others
Alabama	7	7	Montana	7	11
Alaska	2	4	Nebraska	1	1
Arizona	6	1	Nevada	1	1
Arkansas	6	1	New Hampshire	2	2
California	44	58	New Jersey	14	6
Colorado	12	8	New Mexico	5	8
Connecticut	9	4	New York	29	64
Delaware	1	0	North Carolina	8	17
District of Col.	13	9	North Dakota	3	1
Florida	12	2	Ohio	19	3
Georgia	7	12	Oklahoma	2	–
Hawaii	2	1	Oregon	9	11
Idaho	2	4	Pennsylvania	18	3
Illinois	20	8	Rhode Island	2	–
Indiana	4	–	South Carolina	4	7
Iowa	9	1	South Dakota	5	3
Kansas	4	–	Tennessee	7	17
Kentucky	7	4	Texas	22	16
Louisiana	10	3	Utah	2	1
Maine	–	4	Vermont	3	2
Maryland	8	3	Virginia	6	6
Massachusetts	11	13	Washington	11	16
Michigan	10	1	West Virginia	2	2
Minnesota	18	13	Wisconsin	13	5
Mississippi	6	4	Wyoming	2	1
Missouri	6	2	Puerto Rico	5	

esting comparisons could be made between the six funders in my sample, some of the larger endowed private foundations, the Funding Exchange's family of public foundations that also make progressive social change grants, and the many church-related social justice funding organizations. Until then the data in this chapter and the examples of grants by category in the next will have to stand alone.

Analysis of recent CHD granting patterns

Because CHD's annual reports code each grant in a number of different ways, some further intuitions can be developed from the set of reports for the eight-year period, 1980–1987, that

CHD provided for my research. Each grant is placed in what they call a "technical category" and also described in terms of race and ethnic focus and urban or rural location.

The technical categories used by CHD to describe the subject matter for each project are the following:

1. communications
2. economic development
3. education
4. health
5. housing
6. legal aid
7. social development

Table 7.3 is my tabulation of CHD grants by technical category over the 1980–1987 period, as given in CHD's annual reports. Figure 7.1 charts dollar volumes of grants for the total array and the social development category.

Figure 7.1 also shows that CHD collections from the parishes did not increase steadily in the 1980s, but they may be expected to match or exceed the best years of the past now that CHD has been given its permanent status. The graph provides little evidence that the Tax Reform Act of 1986, which lowered tax rates, decreased the attractiveness of giving to tax-exempt causes. The tax deductibility of contributions to CHD may never have been a factor, in any case, because the average contribution by parishioners was relatively small compared to the average size of contribution to the other foundations in my sample.

Figure 7.2, using CHD's categories, shows the distribution of the grants other than for social development over the 1980–1987 period.

As shown in Figure 7.1, grants in the social development category dominate the array. The extremely brief descriptions of projects in the reports of the five other foundations provided only occasional clues as to the racial or ethnic populations being served, so I was particularly interested in seeing how the CHD projects were distributed. My cross-tabulation of the 442 grants made by CHD in 1986 and 1987 by ethnic composition as noted

Table 7.3
Analysis of Projects Funded by CHD, 1980–1987 (in Thousands of Current Dollars)

Technical Category	1980	1981	1982	1983	1984	1985	1986	1987
1 Communications	373	333	97	272	220	125	69	115
2 Economic Development	407	327	367	455	510	347	657	674
3 Education	235	120	165	138	120	225	187	62
4 Health	0	0	0	0	0	0	40	0
5 Housing	626	668	284	415	414	392	381	652
6 Legal Aid	572	405	443	616	233	149	188	104
7 Social Development	3,217	3,659	5,042	5,635	5,509	5,208	4,818	4,887
Total	5,430	5,512	6,398	7,530	7,006	6,445	6,340	6,494
Average total grant	41	36	33	34	32	30	29	30
Average Soc.Dev.grant	39	36	32	33	32	30	29	30

Figure 7.1
CHD Grants: Total and Social Development, 1980–1987

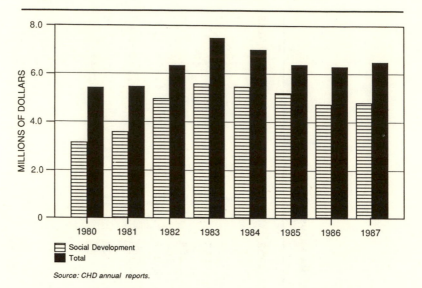

Source: CHD annual reports.

by CHD and by subject matter according to my eight-fold list is seen in Table 7.4.

Table 7.4 shows clearly the emphasis that CHD places on community organizing, economic activities, and housing-related projects for its ethnic grantees. Many of the projects it considers multiethnic are color-blind or in well-integrated neighborhoods or rural areas. The table also suggests that CHD is relatively uninterested in environmental and educational reforms, but, in fact, such concerns often are central to the community organizing campaigns it supports.

Intermediate grantees and networking

One of the important functions that progressive social change philanthropies perform is the funding of a bevy of policy institutes and public information centers, most of which are located, for obvious reasons, in the nation's capital. Such grantees are

Figure 7.2
CHD Grants by Technical Category, 1980–1987

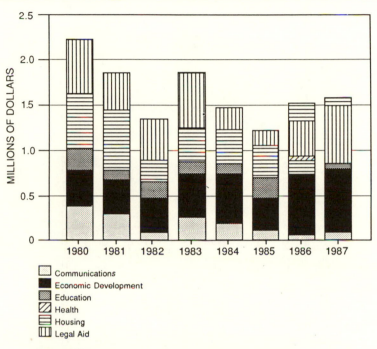

Communications
Economic Development
Education
Health
Housing
Legal Aid

Source: CHD reports.

ordinarily directed and staffed by professionals, often working on behalf of disadvantaged groups but not controlled by them.

Many progressive funders concentrate their donations on one area of passionate interest, often having to do with the physical environment. Each area of interest contains a number of intermediate grantees that can be supported with larger than average grants, for the funds available to any given organization are rarely sufficient for the level of programming desired, given the high costs of national campaigns.

In any case, such intermediate grantees typically violate a criterion (such as CHD's) that a disadvantaged group should be the dominant voice in the operation, but every rule has its exceptions. CHD in 1987, for instance, funded projects at nine

Table 7.4
Distribution of CHD Grants by Subject and Ethnic Group, 1986–1987 (Number of Grants)

(number of grants)

Subject Group (short titles)	Native Amer.	Asian	Black	Hispanic	Multi-Ethnic*	White	Total
1. Community organizing	1	-0-	28	24	60	41	154
2. Economic justice	10	2	3	4	15	7	41
3. Economic security	10	3	16	16	24	48	117
4. Housing/Comm. Dev.	-0-	1	21	7	36	10	75
5. Environment	-0-	-0-	-0-	-0-	2	6	8
6. People and Health	-0-	-0-	2	-0-	9	27	38
7. Schools and media	-0-	-0-	1	2	1	1	9
8. Internat'l affairs	-0-	-0-	-0-	-0-	-0-	-0-	-0-
Total	25	6	71	53	147	140	442

* includes grants coded by CHD as multi-ethnic, black/white, black/hispanic, hispanic/white, etc.

such national organizations: Rural Coalition's Native American Task Force, Citizens Clearinghouse for Hazardous Waste's outreach program, National Training and Information Center's program to foster partnerships between local banks and community organizations, Project Vote!, Americans for Health's national health care campaign, National Community Service Fund's program to foster local minority-controlled alternatives to existing community-chest campaigns, the Affiliated Media Foundation Movement, the Central American Refugee Center's legal-advocacy program, and the National Union of the Homeless. Except for the omission of the more outspoken civil-rights advocates and a variety of peace advocates and critics of American foreign and military policies, CHD's short list of national organizations is reasonably representative of the much longer list of such enterprises funded by the other foundations in my sample.

Actually, slightly over half of the 1,040 grants made by these five foundations were to nationally- or internationally-oriented organizations rather than to local or grass-roots organizations. The number of organizations funded is somewhat lower than the number of grants because several of these foundations network by funding the same project, sometimes successively over the years.

The hundreds of names of such intermediary grantees that appear in my list need not be printed here, but reference should be made to *Winning America: Ideas and Leadership for the 1990s*, an extraordinary review of progressive causes assembled in 1988 by Marcus Raskin and Chester Hartman at the Institute for Policy Studies.[2] Their book includes the names and addresses of the leading policy-oriented organizations connected with each of the many diverse issues discussed.

All these nongrass-roots think tanks and public-issue centers are part of the networking process by which "thinking globally" is linked by funders to the opportunity to "act locally" and make a wider public aware of how a national issue affects their own local social or economic environment.

In a larger sense, networking is a vital characteristic of funding and fund-raising. Funders talk among themselves and suggest new sources to their grantees, while grantseekers search the directories of grant-making organizations for foundations with promising guidelines.

Grantmakers have a variety of techniques for trading information among themselves concerning promising grantees. The more traditional foundations have established national and regional associations. The social change community is served by the National Network of Grantmakers and, on a less organized basis, by the Funding Exchange's Council on National Priorities, both of which invite hundreds of funders and grantees to meet together from time to time to discuss emerging issues that merit grants for policy studies and grass-roots organizing. The Funding Exchange itself is a network of public foundations in which funding decisions are made by boards of grass-roots representatives rather than by the relatively wealthy donors.

Some funders write guidelines, sit back, and wait for proposals. Some actively encourage proposals from selected organizations. On occasion, a few grantmakers conclude that grantees have bypassed an issue of importance, and so a group of funders may institute a program of grants focused on their chosen issue, for example, the policies of the United States in Central America, and will recruit other funders to follow suit. Consequently, sometimes grants flow from a network of foundations and individuals to a select handful of qualified grantees, some of which may have been created for the purpose.

The 1,482 grants from the six foundations in my database provide some original evidence of the extent to which such networking takes place. From the full list of grantees, I selected for analysis those that had received funding from more than one of the six foundations. While the results of the analysis are suggestive concerning the way the system of progressive social change philanthropy operates, they are hardly definitive. One reason is that many individuals make annual contributions to one or more of the six foundations surveyed. Moreover, the sample itself is heavily weighted by the inclusion of two funding years for the Campaign for Human Development and the Youth Project, although these two grantmakers can be cited as exemplary in the social change community.

The entries below are only suggestive of the networking process. Inclusion of a score of other major funders (such as the

New World and Veatch Foundations) and data for other years would change the conclusions in unknown ways. The vast database on grants compiled by the Foundation Center covers only foundations disbursing more than $1 million annually and thus excludes the hundreds, or thousands, of social change funders of more modest means who would have to be identified and surveyed to provide a more accurate picture.

For a variety of project grants other than type 8 (national security, peace, etc.):

- CHD and the Youth Project funded twenty-three organizations together.
- CHD and the Youth Project and/or JFS, Tides, and Threshold funded seven organizations together.
- The Youth Project and JFS funded twenty-seven organizations together.
- The Youth Project and JFS and/or Tides and Threshold funded four organizations together.
- The Youth Project or JFS and/or Tides, Threshold, and the Women's Foundation funded six organizations together.

For a variety of peace and security (type 8) projects (none funded by CHD):

- The Youth Project and JFS funded twelve organizations together.
- The Youth Project and Tides funded one organization together.

Grantmaking organizations receiving a number of grants (mostly donor-directed) from one or more of the six foundations in my sample:

- The Youth Project received six grants for its projects from JFS and two grants from Tides.
- The Tides Foundation received four grants from the Youth Project and one from Threshold Foundation.
- The Threshold Foundation received one grant from the Tides Foundation.
- The Funding Exchange received one grant from the Tides Foundation.
- McKenzie River Gathering received one grant from the Youth Project.
- MS Foundation received one grant from the Youth Project and four grants from JFS.
- The Network Foundation received one grant from the Tides Foundation.

- The North Star Fund received two grants from the Youth Project.
- The Peace Development Fund (including the Pacific Peace Fund) received four grants from the Youth Project, six from JFS, and one each from Tides and Threshold.
- Ploughshares Fund received four grants from the Youth Project and one each from Tides and Threshold.
- The Seventh Generation Fund received six grants from the Youth Project, five from JFS, three from Tides, and two from Threshold.

The analyses in this chapter have not provided any insights either into the length of time that a given grantee or class grantee remains on the funding dockets of the various philanthropic organizations or into the life cycle of community-based or national organizations. Some aspects of these dimensions of social change philanthropy are discussed in the next two chapters, but, under the best of circumstances, the likelihood is that many of the carefully selected grantees in my list of 1,482 grantees will have faded away, either because of success in fulfilling a topical mission or failure to attract sufficient amounts of technical assistance and financial support. The impetus to social activism in the eight broad subject areas that currently typify the field will remain, however, and a new generation of grantees will undoubtedly emerge to replace those that disappear.

Part Four

Risk Analysis and the Funding Decision

How Funders Make Their Decisions

Actors and Activities in a Funding Cycle

A certain amount of mystery surrounds the entire social change funding system because decisions are made in private. The purpose of this chapter is to provide further insights into how the process works in a hypothetical but reasonably representative funding organization. To that framework, I have added comments on how funders deal with the risks and uncertainties inherent in an "investment" in social change activities, and how they and their client grantees evaluate the funding system.

The funding cycle is the name given to the drama of funding. The actors are the decisionmakers (either boards of directors of a foundation or individual donors), the supporting cast of professional staffers, and the representatives of the prospective grantees. The action is contemporary over the funding cycle and begins with the announcement that proposals are welcome and ends with the successful applicant receiving a check. The script varies from one funding source to another, each one determining its own rules of procedure.

My hypothetical play involves a group of decisionmakers and a small staff of one or two persons. Many funding organizations consist of a major donor, a few members of the family, the family lawyer, and no staff. At the other extreme are the very large foundations with hierarchies of decision-making and extensive staffs. In the middle is the kind of funder used here as example. What qualifies the decisionmakers to act their part in the unfolding drama are strong interest and access to money. As noted elsewhere, they tend to be white, well educated, and often gainfully employed in a profession or business. Somewhere in their upbringing or later experience, they acquired the requisite desire to devote part of their life and some of their wealth to progressive social change philanthropy. Their ages reflect their circumstances, younger grantmakers often dealing with inherited wealth, older ones more able to contribute from their own earnings. Each has a unique story to explain how he or she was attracted to the field, some being appointed to the board of an endowed foundation, others joining a community of like-minded souls donating annually to a public foundation.

The stage for the funding cycle is set by the criteria and guidelines adopted by the organization at an earlier time. My hypothetical funders are using the basic criteria issued by the Campaign for Human Development, as discussed in Chapter 6. This means that almost all of the proposals on the docket involve grass-roots organizing by applicants controlled by members of minority or low-income groups. By the same token, none of the proposals are for supplements to governmental grants; for services such as health clinics, soup kitchens, or Boy Scout troops; for a professor's research project; or for a university's building fund.

Most of the decisionmakers of this hypothetical group have had some apprenticeship in grant-making as junior members of their boards, and some may have served as staff or organizers for social change groups or foundations. In addition, they may have read such books as Johnson's *The First Charity*. Johnson's first admonition to funders is that they be clear as to what results they are looking for, what functions the grantee is to perform with the grant, and what organizational strengths the grantee needs to carry out its program.[1] At the very least, he suggests that funders establish some working criteria by which to evaluate proposals from the field. His list of criteria has funders assuring themselves that the prospective grantee has established its legitimacy in its own community, has a defined focus to its program along with demonstrated competence, and encourages both broad participation and leadership development in its constituency.

Johnson also emphasizes that funders have a range of choice regarding the types of grants and grantees; grants can be large or small, for short-term or long-term projects, for established programs or new ones, on big issues or little ones, for single or multiple issues, and, of course, for special projects or for general support of operations.

A more pragmatic set of guidelines comes from the pen of Drummond Pike, president of the Tides Foundation, based on his two decades of experience with the network of social change philanthropists.[2] The guidelines he offers to both funders and grantees include strictures that (a) the proposed grant be more than 5 and less than 50 percent of a grantee's revenues, (b) the grantee gets at least one-third of its revenues from small donations or membership fees and has at least a six-months' reserve in the bank, and (c) the board and staff of the grantee are organized and reasonably stable. He cautions funders to be aware that new organizations, if successful at all, tend to have a tough first year, followed by two years of growth and then two years of relative ease; the problem for funders is to ascertain where the prospective grantee is in its development cycle. Pike emphasizes that site visits and some questioning of disinterested observers of the grantee are indispensable to sound decision-making.

Pike also provides a framework to analyze the financial situation of the applicant grantee. He writes, "The importance of evaluating an organization's financial statements cannot be underestimated. Many times serious management issues, or the lack of program planning, are not evident in well-written proposals, but they are clear after a few simple calculations from the balance sheet."[3] And I note here that funders must get confirmation that the grantee has paid up all its federal and other tax liabilities, for neglecting to do so has been a frequent cause of financial difficulties in ill-managed grass-roots organizations.

Experienced funders can easily add to Pike's list of measures that can be taken to improve the effectiveness of the granting process and to increase the effectiveness of the grantees themselves. Drafting guidelines and criteria is only a beginning, sometimes to be followed by missionary work to create a suitable grantee for the funder's preferred cause and always followed by site visits after appropriate screening of applications. All of the work of evaluation prior to making a grant may, in fact, be far more valuable than evaluation after the fact.

The first act, after the stage is set, is to secure applications for funding from the field. A few proposals may have been invited from groups that met the funding guidelines and that came to the attention of one of the board members or staffers. The majority of these proposals probably came from groups that had received grants in earlier funding cycles. A few others were written because the applicant had discovered by word of mouth or library research that the foundation might be amenable to a proposal if stated procedures were followed.

My hypothetical funder received about forty proposals by the cutoff date that had been established. The sums requested were in the prescribed range of $5,000–$20,000, as stated in the foundation's guidelines. Actually, only a very few large foundations can afford to fund as many as forty grants, and even fewer funders provide support to grass-roots organizations in the $50,000 or more range. At the other extreme, a few social change philanthropists limit their grants to less than $1,000. A very large grant to a fledgling grantee may divert its attention away from the need to develop multiple sources of financial support, and many funders abide by Pike's rule that no grant be less than 5 or more than 50 percent of the grantee's budget.

The second act sees the decisionmakers whittling the list of forty proposals down to a manageable number. One of the responsibilities of the staff is to deflect proposals that do not fit the foundation's guidelines, but sometimes an unsuitable proposal survives such a first cut. More to the point, the aggregate dollar amount for the forty proposals may be two or three times the amount of money the foundation has allocated for distribution during this funding cycle, so that the weakest proposals need to be eliminated before the critical decisions are made. Moreover, the list of site visits has to be small enough to handle efficiently in the limited time available.

During the intermission that follows the initial review, the staff and at least some of the decisionmakers visit each of the applicants that survived the screening process. This is the rule at my hypothetical foundation, for experience has shown that much is learned about what a proposal is all about by talking in the grantee's own environment with its staff and leadership. Even more important is the sense of participation and even exhilaration that usually comes to the foundation director after a visit to an interesting applicant who is putting grants to work in a democratic community. Site visits bring to life the ideas and ideals that are locked into the paragraphs and financial tables of a grant proposal.

Site visits are costly in time and dollars, especially if a foundation entertains proposals on a regional or national basis, but they are essential in minimizing risk and in maximizing mutual learning and involvement along the various actors in the progressive social change networks. Unfortunately, many foundations do not require site visits in their granting process. But, many of the decisionmakers in the progressive public foundations are able to arrange their schedules around the necessity to make such visits.

The final act in the grant-making process is deciding which of the proposals on the scaled-down docket should be selected, how much money should be given, and any conditions to be reflected in the contract that will later be written between the foundation and the successful applicant. The objective information about the proposal comes from the proposal itself and is further expanded by information gained in the site visit. The subjective evaluation of the merits of the proposal is naturally of paramount importance, for each decisionmaker and staffer may have strong feelings about each of the grantees and even stronger opinions as to whether the foundation should be preferring one topic or technique over another.

The day that the final grant-making decisions are made can be full of drama. The docket now contains one proposal in each of the categories described in this book's Appendix. Decisionmaker A has become tired of proposals for organizing a community around local environmental issues and wants the foundation to give more money to grantees working on women's issues and on Native American rights. B is a little sulky because several interesting proposals concerning day-care centers and child abuse have been screened out. C is no longer in favor of giving money to statewide multi-issue organizing campaigns. D has serious doubts that the staff of a proposed grantee is as capable as other decisionmakers believe. E is concerned that the foundation is giving too many grants to inner-city organizations and not enough to rural low-income groups.

The time for decisionmaking arrives. Up on the blackboard in the conference room of my hypothetical foundation go the proposals, listed vertically, and the names of the voting members across the top. The resulting matrix provides a space for each decisionmaker to distribute the total amount of dollars to be given away during this funding cycle among the various proposals. On the first round, some proposals get zeros, some get the requested amount of money. And then the bargaining among the decisionmakers begins, lasting until all agree that a fair distribution has been made of the available funds. In the process, a few grantees come away with nothing, others with less than they requested. And the decisionmakers have had one more learning experience in the arts of deal-making and compromise. Curtain.

Making Grantees Accountable

As the curtain falls on the granting process, it rises on the process of administering the grant. To the staff is delegated the work of negotiating a contract with each successful grantee. Such a contract specifies the purposes for which and the conditions under which the grant is made, how the money is to be delivered, and what kinds of interim reports are required.

A certain amount of angst pervades the offices of most progressive social change funders, doubts as to whether they are funding the right organizations or causes in the first place, and uncertainties as to the effectiveness and survivability of the selected grantees. And there are necessary precautions to be taken to make sure that funds are not used for purposes not envisaged in the contract.

Some of the fears that grants might be misappropriated by grantees are based on newspaper reports over the decades since the Great Society programs of the 1960s began to fund all sorts of groups dealing with poverty issues. Federal funds were augmented by state and local grant programs and by local community-chest and foundation grants. Many of the executives of the receiving agencies, some of whom were from minority populations, were inexperienced in administering large agencies and were often inadequately supervised or audited. To these fears can be added the realization that vast amounts of governmental funds are siphoned off illegally or at least unconscionably by sophisticated people, as the revelations over the years of defalcations and improper political payoffs in the federal military and housing programs illustrate.

The saving grace in the field of progressive social change philanthropy is that most of the grass-roots organizations or think tanks are relatively small operations and thus the amounts of funds from any one donor to any given organization are equally small and manageable. Budgets for these organizations rarely exceed a few hundred thousand dollars a year from all sources. These sums can be compared to the multimillion dollar budgets of major service-delivery or welfare agencies, with hundreds of employees and thousands of clients.

A well-established social change grantee will probably have its own nonprofit 501(c)(3) corporate identity, and it will be able to provide its funders with audited financial statements to supplement its other budgetary information. Even so, funders may ask a grantee to improve internal financial management skills. Among other services offered to its grantees, the Youth Project provides consulting by a financial expert. In the case of a newly formed grantee without its own corporate identity, the funders ordinarily require that the grantee find an established tax-exempt organization that agrees to act as a fiscal agent, accountable to the funder for the proper administration of the granted funds being passed through to the fledgling organization.

To the foundation's staff fall most of the chores of administering grants and reporting back to the foundation's board and its funders from the end of the decision-making process to the beginning of the next funding cycle. Taking positive steps to improve the effectiveness of grants to grass-roots organizations has turned out to be far more difficult than evaluating the effectiveness of a think tank, whose reports can be weighed and discussed and whose policy recommendations can be seen to have been either adopted or ignored by the general public and its elected representatives.

One question that arises at this point is whether any grant can be equitably and efficiently monitored. Charles Merrill suggests that the grantee should be left alone (see Chapter 9); perhaps he is right, for there are few ways to measure the extent to which the expectations of a funder can be matched by the performance of the grantee and even fewer ways to measure the extent to which society has been improved or long-term change effected by such grants. Is it the growth and stability of the grantee that is important? Is it the number of other funding organizations that follow suit? Is it the number of laws passed or elections won? Is it the amount of newspaper coverage or favorable editorial comment? Can an estimate even be made of the number of low-income or minority or disdvantaged or environmentally threatened citizens who have been affected by the granting program?

At a more modest level of evaluative monitoring, funders may urge the staffs and boards of directors of the grantees to accept technical assistance and training either in addition to or in lieu of a grant. A goodly number of books have been written on the subject, especially on fund-raising and administration, and a number of educational institutions offer courses in the care and feeding of nonprofit enterprises.[4]

Staff training and the survivability of a given grantee have a way of surfacing when the subject of multiyear grants for multi-issue grass-roots organizations is raised. Multiyear commitments provide time and resources for a grantee to demonstrate both the validity of its program and its ability to thrive. Thriving, however, often means securing a sounder financial base, which in turn may require further training and technical assistance. Staff turnover, especially with regard to key personnel who may not be able to survive on relatively low salaries and few benefits, is a major obstacle to stability, much less growth, in a grass-roots enterprise.

Multiyear grants to multi-issue organizations, such as Fair Share networks, are an expression of confidence on the part of funders in the choice of issues and their relative emphasis on the part of the grantee. Some funders are troubled by both the extent of the financial commitment and the difficulty of keeping track of multiple initiatives by a given grantee. Nevertheless, funders are often told by their grantees that their mutual effectiveness will be enhanced by generous use of the technique of multiyear funding.

Just as the concept of an informal progressive social change philanthropic network implies communication and collaboration between a number of funders and a number of grantees (together with assorted pundits, scholars, and politically involved citizens) so does the concept of the funding cycle imply a good deal of mutuality and respect between decisionmakers, professional staffers, and the managers and directors of the grantee. Evaluation and monitoring of each grant is essential to the process. And, as one funding cycle follows another, the urge to see the forest instead of the individual trees may come to the fore. The next chapter takes up the question of the efficacy of the process itself.

How Funders Evaluate Their Work

Measuring the Costs and Benefits of Grants

Only an Ebenezer Scrooge or a dedicated social Darwinist would cast doubt upon the ethical or moral basis for all the vision and effort that are displayed by the progressive social change philanthropic network. But Americans are pragmatists at heart and want the security of knowing that their time and money are well spent. And so most funders like to take as hard a look as possible, using the most sophisticated tools available, to evaluate what they are doing, in short, to determine if the costs the funders and grantees bear are worth the benefits they have created.

Cost-benefit analysis in various forms became a standard technique in public and private management during the post–World War II decades. Under its umbrella are the classic form used in evaluating water-power and highway programs; President Johnson's espousal of planning-programming-budgeting systems (PPBS) in federal agencies; the use of discounted cash flows by industrialists contemplating capital investment programs; impact assessments of proposed developments by local governments; and federal evaluations of new drugs, environmental standards, and proposed corporate mergers. The generic problem in the application of any form of cost-benefit analysis to real world problems is the measurement of nonmonetary effects on individuals and groups in the affected population.

Measuring the effect of any social program pushes the art and science of cost-benefit analysis to its limits. At the very least, it requires the creation of some nonmonetary effect (e.g., satisfaction, inconvenience, or increase in mobility or interaction) that can be denominated, scaled, and handled in an evaluation matrix. The question here is the extent to which the work of progressive social change philanthropists either over the past three decades or for any shorter period is amenable to such an approach.

Asking whether funders' dollars have generated long-lasting social changes or made any real difference to any low-income and minority groups or improved chances for ecological survival or peace is like asking the question "Did the War on Poverty Fail?" In a 1989 editorial with that title, Hyman Bookbinder, executive officer of President Lyndon Johnson's Task Force on Poverty in 1964, answered, "No, it didn't; society did."[1] His argument, briefly, is that our society "tired of the war too soon, gave it inadequate resources and did not open up new fronts as required," and he noted some of the permanent gains: universal acceptance of the need for a "social 'safety net' " and a score of enduring programs such as Head Start, Job Corps, Community Action, Medicare, and Medicaid. He asked some questions not usually addressed by those who are skeptical of the objects of progressive philanthropy:

Has every defense contract yielded a perfect product, at minimum cost? Has every cancer project brought a cure? Has every space launching succeeded? Has every diplomatic initiative brought peace? Why should a less than perfect record for social programs be less tolerable to society than failed economic, military or diplomatic policies?

The foundation trustees and executives and the staffs of their grantees that I have worked with over the years generally share Bookbinder's sentiments, even as they accept the inherent limitations of the efforts at social change. If required, they can measure the costs in terms of dollar amounts of grants made and overhead carried, together with millions of hours of unpaid or low-paid labor. I have found that they believe strongly that such costs are more than justified by the social benefits they helped create, as measured by the number of community residents who have become inspired and involved, by environmental and peace movements that have become a permanent part of the national consciousness, and, more recently, by some withdrawal from the excessive narcissism and greed that characterized American society in the 1970s and 1980s.

Nevertheless, as with all social programs, continuing efforts at self-evaluation and subsequent improvements in operating methods are all to the good. The main theme I find emerging from such a process is that a pound of prevention is worth a pound of cure, in the sense that care taken in the making of a grant is worth more than post hoc evaluation of the success or failure of a project.

Funders learn to deal in a positive fashion with the uncertainties of their profession. Moreover, funding is fun, in spite of the doubts, and I imagine that the typical foundation trustee or executive looks back with pride and pleasure at his or her good works over years of service. I have not made an exhaustive search for such retrospective writings, but my favorite to date is Charles Merrill's *The Checkbook*. A few comments abstracted from that unique book suffice to set the stage for further discussion of how funders seek to improve the effectiveness of their grants.

With few exceptions, we [trustees] did not hire outside experts to examine a field or a project we were considering nor to evaluate what we had accomplished. . . . We also rejected almost any articulation of priorities . . . any line of policy that suggested constraint was listened to and then ignored. . . . [Our] form of scattered, ad hoc, old-boy-network way of doing business is despised by critics of establishment foundations as the reason why their expenditures, on the whole, don't have much effect. To an extent I agree [but] I go back and forth between a belief in discipline and an acceptance of serendipity. . . . If we made some dumb mistake, we hoped that the money was not completely wasted, and we would try to do better next time.

Waldemar Nielsen's *The Big Foundations* (commissioned by the Twentieth Century Fund and first published in 1972 by Columbia University) is an excellent study of the thirty-three American foundations with assets exceeding $100 million. Nielsen criticizes these foundations for their timidity, lethargy, self-serving and self-praise, as well as often simple mismanagement. The Merrill Trust was well run and honestly run, but I recognize ourselves in his criticisms.

We issued no reports. We were unimpressed by the theory of accountability. It was *our* money. Annual reports would have exposed us to even more seagulls squalling around a stranded whale. We scorned the glossy-brochure puffery of other foundations praising their social goodness. Now I believe that a report every two or three years would have been useful in forcing us to measure what we had done and might do.[2]

In contrast, most funders do feel accountable, although they may not be quite sure to whom. The Campaign for Human Development did not have that problem. CHD acts from a firm base in church teachings, but it needed a long evaluation of its accomplishments and methods in order to become a permanent part of the United States Catholic Conference's mission. The required and affirming assessment was performed by the Bishops' Oversight Committee, and CHD's ad hoc status was accordingly removed in November of 1988.[3]

The Oversight Committee, while validating CHD's past performance, saw the need for improving operations in a number of ways, including more emphasis on educating Catholics concerning the church's social doctrines and thereby increasing the annual collection. A key element in the strategies recommended for the future was the finding that "CHD should continue to use economic development as a means to empower the poor and should concentrate its economic development resources on the creation of successful models which foster participatory control and ownership for low-income people.[4]

Other progressive social change funders seem to have more difficulty in deciding what activities to support. At their annual retreats, they engage in a continuing search for effective causes. Their lists change from year to year, with energy and the environment prominent at one time, perhaps to be followed by greater interest in peace movements, voter education and registration, child welfare, civil rights, and, of course, methods of increasing economic security. One popular technique to narrow their options and deepen their understanding of the issues of the day is to support research and policy formation at think tanks across the nation, followed by support of training and public education regarding the policy recommendations.

Only a few foundations or individuals in the field of progressive philanthropy have the resources to make their own detailed assessments of the effectiveness of particular one-year or multiyear grants. Over the years, of course, leading philanthropic organizations such as the Ford, Carnegie, and Russell Sage Foundations and the Twentieth Century Fund, have commissioned studies by their own staffs and their learned consultants on the efficacy of various social programs. The typical funder, I suspect, relies heavily on the self-evaluations of past and present performance provided by hopeful grantees in their funding proposals. These proposals, possibly supplemented by site visits, are carefully reviewed on a case-by-case basis and then compared with competing applications at the ensuing grant-making session. One funding cycle follows another using the grantmaker's established guidelines, until the time the funder stands back to reconsider and revise those published guidelines that had generated such an unceasing flow of applications. Only rarely have progressive funders had the kind of opportunity, reviewed in the following section, that was provided to David Hunter to consider the effectiveness of a whole generation's worth of funding experience.

" . . . If I Had It to Do over Again"

David H. Hunter, who became the guru of a whole generation of progressive social change funders while serving as executive director of the Stern Fund for more than a quarter of a century until its termination in 1987, provided a thoughtful evaluation of the successes and failures of social change funding in a speech entitled " . . . if I had it to do over again." The speech was delivered to the annual National Network of Grantmakers conference and symbolizes the beginning of the present age of uncertainty about the directions of social change after decades of less modest assertions.[5]

The theme of the conference was sustaining the capacity for change, but Hunter's assessment of the situation was that the progressive social change movement needed far more vision and devotion to the necessity for systemic change than he had observed. The people at the conference, he said, had access to money and influence and thus bore a particular responsibility to stem the tide of reactionary events.

The defenders of privilege can fight hard, too. . . . Anti-democratic people are sitting in the seats of power, and they are not just sitting there. They are changing things. Social change, if you will, but not the kind of social change we had in mind when we started to use that term.

As he urged foundations to question existing activist practices and to fortify themselves with "some ideals beyond materialistic individualism and jingoism, some explicitly stated values that would help us move toward a more democratic and egalitarian society," he also recognized that new visions risked upsetting traditionalists among the funders.

Obviously, a serious effort of this kind will challenge some sacred cows and gore some oxen. How much of our destiny can we leave to market forces? How much gap between haves and have nots can a society that pretends to be a democracy tolerate? Should there be limits to the wealth any person should have or control? How much can and should national sovereignty be limited? Questions like these stir the blood. But why shouldn't foundations help to raise and explore them.

If we are to make headway toward the fundamental changes all those people are talking about, there needs to be some heavy thinking, heavy thinking not restricted by conventional models, not restrained by taboos, not governed exclusively by the guidelines of the "art of the possible." Foundations should self-consciously and explicitly support serious work by people, organizations and institutions undertaking radical research and design. If they are uncomfortable about this they can say: "Of course *we* don't really believe this stuff but in an open society radical critique should have access to the stage as much as conservative or non-controversial efforts."

" . . . if I had it to do over again," I would do more of that. Who knows, some challenging new perspectives might grow out of an ambience less intellectually cramped and ideologically restricted. At the very least we might be spared some of the vagueness and double-talk to which we are exposed now.

Another area in which I think we are somewhat deficient is our failure too often to think and act systematically, to take *systems transformation* as our target rather than amelioration of the symptoms of system malfunctioning.

Too many funders, he added, were engaged in negative thinking merely to stem the tide of reaction and, equally to be regretted, were thinking with limited vision in less-than-systemic ways, in contrast to the intellectual vigor with which some exemplary activists were developing fresh approaches to endemic problems in housing, national security, and Central American affairs.

To his mind, foundations needed to avoid being elitist, needed to identify more closely with their grantees, and needed to be careful not to subvert the possibility of systemic change as an unintended result of only funding less controversial programs. Even as he urged the leaders of the foundation community to get into the trenches, he concluded:

Not many of the final decisionmakers in foundations are people who believe that our society is in need of "fundamental change." Not many decisionmakers are enthusiastic about public or governmental intervention in the market place. Although this is delicate territory, foundations should face up to it. Some are mature and open enough to discuss it in their boards. It does not get much discussion now.

This is related to the basic question of whether or not in this country we can bring about the changes necessary to improve matters in the direction of social justice and democracy without violence and disruption; whether we can do a better job of providing jobs, decent housing, health care, and not least, international peace, without social chaos forcing *some* kind of action that could well be reactionary, even fascistic, as well as progressive.

And, naturally, he had thoughts about money.

[W]hat organizations *do* has a substantial impact on their capacity to mobilize support. By their penuriousness, social change oriented foundations are forced to be particularly attentive to insuring in so far as it is humanly possible that the recipients of their grants really are change-oriented and not just "good" things. . . . Some of the past sources of that kind of money either have or are in the process of disappearing (e.g. DJB, Field Foundation, Stern Fund). But it's hard for me to believe that there isn't some new money out there to take their place.

Hunter's speech is a long way from the self-praise that Charles Merrill saw emanating from the foundation community, but this chapter shows how tenuous a grip we have on the problem of evaluation of past grants and how difficult it is, using Hunter's terms, to avoid "wallowing" in piles of proposals to help "move the society toward peace, and social and economic justice." Careful evaluation of a proposal reduces the operational risk entailed in any grant to an activist organization, but Hunter also provided this section's capstone by interpreting the concept of risk analysis to mean that funders have a continuing responsibility to increase the social risks inherent in their funding programs.

Stabilizing the System

Long-term Relationships between Grantees and Their Funders

Since practically everyone in the field of progressive funding agrees that it is a risky activity, the burden ultimately falls upon the community organization to be adaptable and persistent on its way to viability. The following comments, including a short case study of Chicago's Citizens Information Service (CIS), which has a distinguished thirty-five-year-long record of gaining wide community support for its efforts, is meant to show that progressive organizations can succeed.

The Citizens Information Service (CIS) in Chicago is a prime example of how a reasonably progressive community organization can survive over an extended period of time. It was established in 1954 to provide citizens with the information they would need to deal effectively with complex and highly politicized county and city governments.[1]

CIS has done a good job of empowering citizens of all ethnic groups and income levels. As such, it tends to get entrenched bureaucrats and judges upset, in a less aggressive manner perhaps than did CIS's even more activist neighbor, Saul Alinsky's Back of the Yards organization, but moderately enough so that CIS gained broad financial support from scores of corporate and community foundations, the local bar associations, and a large number of family funds. CIS may not fit CHD's criteria concerning ownership by low-income or minority people but, in

Figure 10.1
General Support for CIS, 1954–1988 (in Thousands of Dollars)

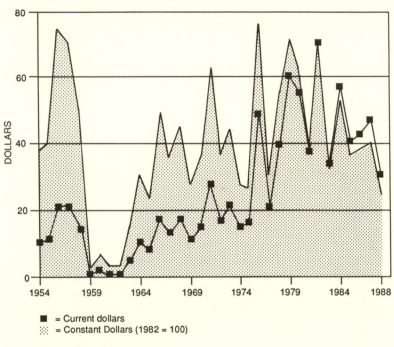

■ = Current dollars
⠿ = Constant Dollars (1982 = 100)

Source: CIS records.

any case, it has not received significant support from church-based organizations.

General support for CIS has come from many sources over the years. Barbara Page Fiske, one of its long-term board members, provided a special tabulation of all donations of $1000 or more over the years, noting that CIS got off to a flying start in its first three years as the beneficiary of a $65,000 grant from the Emil Schwartzhaupt Foundation in New York, the same foundation that had been instrumental in funding the Highlander School's civil rights training program and that was seeking useful ways to disburse its remaining capital just as CIS was starting.

Total receipts from these $1000-and-over donors year by year from its beginning are charted in Figure 10.1 (but note that smaller donations from hundreds of supporters are not included in this tabulation of large donations). After the initial Schwartz-haupt grant, receipts declined (as an example of Drummond Pike's concept of the first five-year cycle for a fledgling organization) until, as the Chinese say, the times became more interesting in the 1960s. The donations continued to climb, with variations caused sometimes by funding patterns convenient to donors, sometimes by the attractiveness of the programs being mounted by CIS. Its financial records reflect changes over time in its list of major donors as a result of death, divorce, and job changes or retirements that carried the donors away from the Chicago area. The record attests to CIS's utility to its community, but, as Figure 10.1 reveals, the growth of its general support by major donors in current dollars is more dramatic than when converted into constant (1982) dollars.

As often happens, however, funds for particular special projects are easier to obtain than general-support funds, and CIS has an enviable record of designing special projects to meet changing needs. Among those highly fundable projects were:

Publications. Its first project was publication of a handbook on Cook County government, *This is Cook County*, followed soon after by the *Key to Chicago Government*. CIS has updated these from time to time and issued many other reports and newsletters.

Training programs and workshops. CIS funded training programs and workshops for such diverse groups as citizen leaders; Spanish-speaking immigrants needing English as a second language and assistance in immigration and naturalization proceedings; parents; school council members; and local citizens wanting more political education, some understanding of governmental budget processes, and better writing skills.

Community Education in Law and Justice (CELJ). Statewide workshops beginning in 1978 on the entire criminal justice system were funded in part by the Illinois Law Enforcement Commission with federal Law Enforcement Assistance Administration (FEAA) funds.

Urban Crime Prevention Program (UCPP). Beginning in 1974, UCPP involved 10 community organizations and was funded in part by the federal Law Enforcement Assistance Administration.

Funds were cut off and subsequently UCPP was funded by the Ford Foundation. It later became an independent organization (Chicago Alliance of Neighborhood Safety), raising its own funds.

Court Watching. With the League of Women Voters, CIS began a project to train observers in court proceedings with a view to improving the process. Subsequently the program became an independent organization, raising its own funds.

CD Memo. CD Memo was a newsletter sent free to community organizations with late updates on community development funding deadlines, budgets, and hearings. It ceased publication when the city began issuing its own publication.

Throughout the 35-year period covered by these data, CIS worked hard to assure its own survival. Over half of CIS's contributors to the general support fund also helped fund one or more of these special projects, or perhaps the appeals for programmatic funds turned contributors into general supporters. Extensive support came from a distinguished group of funders: the Joyce Foundation, the Field Foundation of Illinois, the Ford Foundation, the Chicago Community Trust, the Harris Trust's foundation, and, especially, the Wieboldt Foundation (which only funded programs). The Joyce Foundation is noteworthy for having funded a thorough evaluation of CIS's structure and programs in 1978.

The survival of CIS, according to my source, Barbara Fiske, is a tribute not only to its large donors but also to the smaller financial contributions of hundreds of supporters, to its constant search for useful programs, and especially to its ability to train and inspire generations of volunteer board members. The role of a grass-roots organization's board is sometimes neglected by the grant-making community, and one of the most useful contributions the board can make (in addition to its fund-raising and policy-formulating functions) is to insist that an organization have a long-term strategy for success.

For many individual citizens, participation in the work of a community-based organization, such as CIS (or of a local chapter of a national social change group such as Friends of the Earth, Greenpeace, Physicians/Educators for Social Responsibility, ACLU, or the NAACP) is their primary contribution to a social movement. The danger is that these individuals will become discouraged as the years go by with little proof that their accomplishments are significant. Faced with the same problems of despair, burnout, and dropout, the Social Movement Empowerment Project has developed (on a grander scale than Pike's five-year cycle and the need for regeneration of a local activity) a strategic framework describing the eight stages of successful social movements. The impetus to develop its Movement Action Plan (MAP) stems from observation of the anti-nuclear-energy campaign and other campaigns: "Within a few years after initial success, activists inevitably believe that their movement is failing and their efforts have been futile—even when their movement is satisfactorily progressing along the road of past successful movements."[2]

The concept that long-term strategies, together with persistence and imagination, are necessary for long-term survival applies to local as well as national initiatives on the social change front. Evaluating a potential grantee's strategy for survival is thus an important point to be considered by the careful funder.

How Grantees See the Problem of Effective Survival

A basic question for the progressive social change community is the effectiveness of relatively small grants in building strong organizations at the grass-roots and statewide levels that can work with each other over time to accomplish meaningful changes in social conditions. At issue is the efficacy of the usual practice that leaves a funding organization so busy issuing guidelines, receiving applications, and making site visits that it rarely asks itself whether the process needs to be improved.

One funder attempted to address the endemic issues that surround that question by commissioning a unique survey of its grantees. To some extent, the findings in its report, *Soundings: A Regional Survey of Organizational Needs and Concerns among A Territory Resource Grantees in Idaho, Montana, Oregon, Washington and Wyoming*, conducted by Michael S. Clark, September 1985, can be generalized to the whole field of progressive social change activities.

A Territory Resource, known more familiarly as ATR, was

established in 1977 as a nonendowed public foundation to serve its region. Its forty or so donors contribute about $250,000 each year and make about forty grants in the $5,000–$15,000 range. ATR's donors, together with professional staff and outside directors, make the funding decisions, in contrast to the practice at the public foundations that are members of the Funding Exchange, which requires that a community board representing grass-roots organizations take responsibility for allocating available funds.

After eight years of activity, ATR's board asked Mike Clark, formerly an ATR board member and executive director of the Highlander School in Tennessee and currently executive director of the Environmental Policy Institute, to evaluate the effectiveness of ATR's funding practices by asking a sample of grantees if ATR was meeting their needs. Clark's survey came after the first five years of the Reagan administration, a period that saw many former support programs vitiated and that included significant changes in the resource-based economies, notably in agriculture and the lumbering industries, that characterized ATR's five-state region. It was also a time when the relatively exuberant springtime for progressive social change activities in the 1970s had passed into history, and both the community of funders and the vast diversity of grantees exemplified by the vignettes presented in the Appendix were searching for policies that would build more cohesive and stable progressive movements in the United States.

ATR's goal is to be a resource for organizations attempting to establish a society that is politically and economically democratic, equitable and environmentally sound. Clark's summary findings concerning its first eight years of operation were that:

ATR has built a unique, vital role for itself among social change groups in the region. It serves as an invaluable funding source, especially for young, emerging groups. It also is seen as a key intellectual resource and technical assistance center for grantees and other groups. Increasingly, ATR is viewed as an information resource for groups seeking funds both within and outside the region. . . .

By funding new groups and projects, it often can legitimize an issue or an organization. This process often enhances the ability of groups to successfully raise funds from other sources.

As a stable, regional institution, ATR is uniquely positioned to play a crucial leadership role among activists in the region. For this to take place, ATR must continue to be sensitive to issues of accountability toward both its donors and the constituency of social change groups it has created over the years.[3]

However, Clark found the grantee community facing a set of serious problems, which, unless addressed, would inhibit the future stability and growth of the individual organizations and the creation of a cohesive progressive movement in the region. Underlying these problems were the attempts of the grantees to adapt their tactics and strategies to the "enormous shifts in public policy and in the public's view of how government should function" that characterized the early years of the Reagan administration. Clark noted that:

Many of the groups, faced with rapidly changing national priorities, and a corresponding shift in how state and local governments are functioning, have scrambled to keep their work relevant and effective. Within this context, effective organizing styles and strategies are still emerging. No one style or approach to community organizing is clearly valid in all parts of the region. Indeed there is a strong need for continuous cross-fertilization of ideas and approaches among groups in all five states. . . .

Almost all have been influenced by organizing styles developed out of two waning national movements: labor organizing and civil rights.[4]

Clark did not discuss further the validity of those organizing styles for work in the 1980s and beyond, but many in the field are troubled by the fragility of the results of community organizing using membership campaigns and sometimes house-to-house canvasses to gain support for single-issue protests. The strength of a grass-roots organization is hard to measure under the best of circumstances, but there is little evidence that local organizations have much staying power when they use this organizing style in economic and political climates that change from year to year.

What Clark did find was that most of ATR's former and current grantees were experiencing major financial problems and that some could not survive without major changes in their programs and in their fund-raising efforts. He also noted that they were not helped by constant changes in a foundation's objectives.

Private foundations sometimes appear to fund in trendy waves, depending upon what is "hot" or "in" among influential East Coast foundations. . . .

Fundraising strategies strongly influence how a social change organization functions, how it carries out planning activities, how it remains accountable to its constituencies (funders are a crucial element of any constituency base), and how it copes with pressures to survive and remain effective.

Leaders of these organizations spend an enormous amount of time dealing with fundraising concerns. Consciously or unconsciously, many social change organizations build a complex array of program assumptions around fundraising strategies. Yet only rarely are these assumptions examined to determine how fundraising affects program goals.

For example, many of the groups dealing with questions of social justice (women, minorities, low-income, neighborhood groups) depend heavily upon church funding. The importance of church support has increased significantly within the region as cut-backs in federal funding have eliminated or curtailed many social service programs.

What are the implications of depending upon church support for local organizing? How do the benefits outweigh the liabilities? How does this support compare to the advantages of seeking major private foundation funding? How does anticipated church support affect future program goals and organizing strategies? Obviously, the answers to these questions (and their importance) will vary a great deal depending upon the focus and constituency base of each group. Many organizations have shifted into dependency or reliance upon one or more of these sources without dealing consciously with these questions.

To use another example, several state-wide and regional organizations depended a great deal on private foundation grants for general support. This reliance upon foundation grants carries with it an operating mode which is common to many groups—foundation proposal deadlines end up as the key factor in setting programmatic goals and time frames for operating programs.[5]

The symbiosis between funder and grantee is intuitively felt but rarely analyzed in the detail seen in Clark's report. While Clark recognizes that external conditions having to do with the economy, the ebb and flow of financial support from governmental and nongovernmental agencies other than foundations, and the rise of one set of causes while others were dropped from foundation agendas all contributed to the indeterminancies confronting the managers of any grass-roots organization, he went on to suggest that the time had come to challenge the assumption that a little seed money and some encouragement was all that was necessary for a foundation to enable a grass-roots enterprise to become viable and to acquire a permanent funding base.

What he saw throughout the region were community-based organizations subject to rapid turnover of staff, many of whom had been forced to leave the field of social activism in order to find better paying jobs with enough stability to enable them to raise families. For these and other reasons, the organizations were finding it difficult to recruit experienced staff, while the human capital of a number of experienced former staff directors was no longer available to the field. Clark's view, as of 1985, is still applicable.

Perhaps this "greying" of Sixties activists and "forced retirement" of even younger organizers is a natural consequence of how decentralized social change movements develop in our society. Even so, to accept the phenomenon as inevitable ensures the loss of skills and insights gained by large numbers of people through hard work on progressive causes over the past twenty years. It may continue to be impossible for many people to find paid work within the social change field.[6]

Clark did not accept the inevitability of administrative chaos. He suggests that ATR and like-minded funders, in addition to making grants directly to organizations, find ways to support a multifaceted program to correct these systemic deficiences. His recommended program includes a wider use of technical-assistance grants for recruiting and training both staff and board members of grass-roots organizations, a continuing series of regional gatherings to discuss operational problems and to reduce feelings of isolation (partly caused by physical distance between groups), and ways of recapturing and reapplying the skills of the experienced but presently inactive organizers scattered across the region.

Clark considered the staffing problem to be at least as impor-

tant as the funding problem for the group of ATR-funded organizations he had surveyed. He also passed on to his client a
number of comments made by those he had interviewed, among
them:

- Rather than playing a role in networking, ATR should establish a
  growth plan for itself . . . for new funds. The best thing it can do is
  to give money to effective groups. . . . It tells us to raise more money,
  so why can't it do the same thing?
- Rather than bring us together, it might be more effective [for ATR to
  translate] our concerns to the rest of the country.
- If I could tell the ATR board one thing, it would be that our major
  problem lies within the nature of progressive [grantee] organizations.
  In one sense, there are too many of them and they hold on to very
  limited turfs. We fight too hard with each other. We hold on to
  fundamental ideas that we don't challenge enough internally. The
  progressive community has bought in to the notion of pluralism and
  we have reached a point where it has become self-defeating. The
  organizations are too diffuse, we are trying to do too many things at
  once. I remain really worried about the number of groups, the nar-
  rowness of focus, the inability to keep track of what is really going
  on.[7]

ATR and the funding community of which it is a part struggle
with the same concerns that are reflected in these comments
from their grantees. Nothing would please the funding organizations more than to have far more contributors to the general
pot available for progressive social change philanthropy so that
the funders do not face, one funding cycle after another, a situation in which they have to turn down two-thirds of the applications they receive and frequently grant less than the amount
an applicant has requested. Both public and private foundations
have expanded their efforts to increase the size of contributions
from existing individual donors and to add new donors to their
membership, which, in many cases, is largely composed of greying sixties activists dealing with inherited wealth.

To be effective in the 1990s, these funders need to attract a
significant number of new contributors from the population of
older individuals holding earned or inherited wealth, as well as
from the younger generations behind them. Unfortunately, they

are finding it difficult to identify people in their twenties and early thirties who have become involved in public service and social causes; the majority of people on the college campuses of the 1980s have been primarily concerned with personal advancement.

The charge by the unidentified interviewee that the funding community has brought into pluralism is well taken, but no clear remedies are at hand. The funders reserve the right to fund or not fund a particular proposal, and they have been known to suggest that a particular activity be undertaken by a newly fashioned or existing nonprofit tax-exempt entity. They do not, however, arrogate to themselves the right to tell a community or a region what kinds or what number of grass-roots organizations should become operational at one time or another. If anything, funders believe in pluralism and in having citizens becoming active participants in a democratic society, and they will undoubtedly continue to distribute their largesse widely in pursuit of such beliefs.

In line with Clark's recommendations for better communication and possibly greater cohesion among social change activists in the field and for more technical assistance and training, ATR has taken some innovative steps in recent years, beginning with increasing the flow of funds for technical assistance grants. Clark, however, had noted the existence of useful providers of such assistance already at work in the region in addition to ATR, including the Youth Project's Western Office, the Northern Rockies Action Group (NRAG), the Center for Community Change's Western Office, the Community Resource Center, the Rural Coalition, the Center for Third World Organizing (CTWO), and the Agape Foundation, together with the Women's Funding Alliance, the Fair Share network, the Montana Alliance for Progressive Policies, and the Northern Plains Resource Council.

From time to time, ATR (sometimes in association with other funders such as the Youth Project) has sponsored gatherings of grantees to discuss a particular issue. Running more than an occasional conference or training session tended to stretch ATR's few staff to their limits and to divert attention from a variety of equally important administrative tasks, and a separate organization was needed for the purpose.

The Western States Center was created to fill the need for
building a progressive community in the West and to serve as
a model for other regions. Its first several years of operation
were financed by a number of individuals, some of whom were
members of ATR. It hopes to become a financially self-sustaining
membership organization over time, with occasional foundation
grants to finance special projects and programs. Its objectives
and regional scope are broader and its methods are designed to
involve a wider constituency than envisioned in Clark's *Soundings* report. Its flavor is described by its executive director, Jeff
Malachowsky, in this quotation from its first newsletter.

"The democratic impulse runs deep in the West—deep like a taproot,
deep like an underground stream."
    That first line of the Western States Center's Mission Statement af-
firms our respect for the progressive threads running throughout Western political history and culture. The Western states today are
remarkable and fertile ground for citizen leaders and grassroots organizations, all working hard for political and economic democracy, social
justice and sound stewardship of our magnificent resources—land,
water, wilderness.
    But when we add them all up, all our efforts, are they enough? We
are spread out across a vast area, and engaged in work of tremendous
diversity. Although there are hundreds, thousands of us who share
common values, progressive values, there are too few opportunities to
share common experiences—across state lines, around different issues,
between cultures, professions and organizations. We work too often in
isolation from each other.
    The Western States Center was founded in 1987 to challenge this
isolation, which we feel holds back the progressive movement in the
West. Working in Oregon, Washington, Idaho, Montana, Wyoming,
Utah and Nevada, we've chosen to start by convening a series of strategy sessions, retreats and training workshops, each involving people
from all over the region. Our vision is of a broad community of activists
and leaders, sharing values and sharing commitment, at work in in-
terlocking networks, overlapping constituencies and complementary
strategies.
    Eighteen months of extensive interviews and consultation with pro-
gressive leaders throughout the Western region gave direction to the
Center's first projects. The small number of events we organized in
1988 clearly tapped a nerve in the region—more than 200 activists at-

tended from over 80 organizations. Our projects for 1989–90 are each designed, in different ways, to continue bringing together different parts of our diverse community, challenging isolation while delivering practical and useful skills and resources.[8]

Although inspired by the Highlander Center in Tennessee, the Western States Center represents a different model, one that may have applicability in other regions of the nation. Its board of directors will largely be composed of community leaders, not foundation executives. It does not intend to be a think tank or to develop policy initiatives on its own. Instead it will try, on the one hand, to provide opportunities for community leaders meeting together to form their own opinions of what new policies are needed and, on the other hand, to be a channel by which the global policy recommendations of academics and the national groups clustered in the District of Columbia and a few other major centers can be applied locally. In any case, the events of the 1980s combined with the "greying" of many of the principal actors in the ranks of progressive social change funders and grantees who had earned their stripes in the battles of the previous decades make adaptation and self-evaluation the order of the day.

Part Five

Politics and Prospects

Populism and the Foundation World

"P" Is for Politics

Aristotle in *The Politics* remarks that a person who can live without getting involved in the politics of a community is either a beast or a god. Social change philanthropists, whether on the left or right, are neither, and so all their ventures into the funding of grass-roots and nationwide causes inevitably and ineluctably have political implications. When foundation politics intersect with electoral politics, semanticists have a field day; the objective of this section is to put some of the recent controversies and activist programs into a broader context of theory and practice. The last section will look at prospects for progressive social change after the electoral disappointments of the 1988 election campaigns.

My first chapter included comments on the ambiguous words that inhibit communication about social change. I have titled this section "P Is for Politics" in view of the descent of political discourse during the 1988 presidential campaign into "letter-calling" (for example, the dreaded "L-word" used in place of name-calling or mudslinging about liberals).

To raise the level of discourse a few notches, I avoid as much as possible the names of political parties such as Republican and Democratic in the following discussion. I suspect that a number of progressive social change philanthropists are enrolled Republicans, possibly members of the group that used to be called liberal Republicans. Perhaps most of the funders described in this book are enrolled Democrats, or maybe most of them are so-called independents, and some undoubtedly are supporters of movements that might become third parties in hopes of becoming major parties. Some might even be as alienated as are most Americans and refrain from voting at all.

"P" might also stand for progressive or Progressive or populist or Populist, just as most of the funders of grass-roots organizations claim to be democrats with a small "d" rather than Democrats. My own theory is that Americans need a better sense of their own political history in order to make sense of the present confusion of labels.

For example, every student used to know that the party system in the United States, with its republican form of government, began with Jeffersonian Republicans opposed to Hamiltonian-style Federalists. Eventually the Republicans became Democratic Republicans and then just Democrats, the party of Andrew Jackson, while the Federalists remained political liberals interested in using governmental powers to foster private economic development, styled themselves as Whigs for a time, and in 1856 became the Republican party. In other countries, a regime espousing the Republicans' kind of liberalism is sometimes called a "social democracy."

By the time the twentieth century began, the Republicans in America were still liberal in the classic sense (and extreme right-wing antigovernmentalists had not yet styled themselves as libertarians). Populism referred to the movements by farmer and labor groups to gain political power to counterbalance the industrialists and their bankers. The Democratic party became associated with the movement that produced antitrust legislation and regulatory commissions, such as the Interstate Commerce Commission. Despite its broad populist base, to which were added ethnic voters, the New Deal was actually liberal, meaning that it used its powers to reorganize and foster private economic enterprise as well as providing public monies to build facilities (such as dams and hydroelectric generators) for use by industry, farmers, and the general public.

The semantic irony is that the Republican party of Presidents Reagan and Bush is still liberal in the same way the term could be applied to the early New Dealers, and so are most present-day foundation trustees and executives. We have already mentioned Waldemar Nielsen's designation of Viguerie and the Moral Majority as "new populists," but, in a sense, the true conservatives at this end of the twentieth century are still the Jeffersonian and Jacksonian small-"d" democrats, especially those philanthropists (including descendents of the Rockefellers and other holders of "old money") funding grass-roots organizing to foster the kind of democratic participation advocated by Johnson in *The First Charity.*

The term, "progressive social change," in any case, now appears to cover all the activities that will stimulate democratic participation at the grass-roots level and in the voting booth. And a really "populist" movement still seems to be one that incorporates farmers, workers, and all sorts of groups economically and socially disadvantaged, if not disenfranchised, by the way in which our political economy operates. Whatever the semantics of the situation, social change has been endemic throughout American history, and social change is recognized and carried out by politicians acting on and through legislatures. The great foundations established by the nineteenth-century industrialists and by their philosophic heirs in the twentieth century felt free to advocate new legislation and the establishment of organizations to continue advocating improvements in the system. Hardly anyone objected at the time.

However, a number of historical trends coalesced in the mid–twentieth century to make such foundation largesse less acceptable on its face and to make foundation trustees skittish about becoming involved in political advocacy. Institutional economists, such as Thorsten Veblen and John R. Commons, showed how bankers and industrialists dominated our economic system, and the Great Depression inspired fresh looks at existing concentrations of economic power.[1] In the early nineteenth century, de Toqueville had seen that the lack of primogeniture in the United States would tend to disperse great fortunes as they descended through the generations, but corporations do not die in the same way as individuals, and the fear mounted that we

were creating an economic autocracy that would create permanent social classes instead of the fluid (Horatio Alger–type) system that we had adopted as our prevailing myth.

The federal income tax, meanwhile, became a central feature
of the nation's fiscal system. Tax rates, which had been relatively
low from the start in 1913, remained high after their steady rise
during World War II. The federal tax code became the bible for
business enterprise, and the tax collectors of the Internal Revenue Service became not only the guardians of the public purse
but the arbiters of what was deductible or exempt from taxation.

Inevitably, the spotlight began to shine on the activities of tax-
exempt private foundations, whose large endowments were forever beyond the reach of inheritance taxes, whose incomes were
exempt from annual taxes, and whose powers of (political) advocacy were unrestrained. In the early 1950s followers of Senator
McCarthy and the House Un-American Activities Committees
hauled foundation executives up to Capitol Hill to defend their
grants to organizations on McCarthy's lists. In a slightly calmer
but equally hostile mood, Representative Patman entered the
scene in the mid-1960s with well-publicized hearings on the
political activities of private foundations, the result of which was
the Tax Reform Act of 1969, a watershed act for the foundation
world.[2]

After 1969, the worlds of business and philanthropy bumped
into one another more than they had before. For example, as a
student at the Harvard Business School in the late 1940s, I was
confronted with at least a thousand case studies of business
enterprises, but I do not recall a single mention of local charitable
contributions by businessmen or their corporations nor any consideration of the operations of tax-exempt enterprises or foundations. Nor do I remember anyone questioning the propriety,
much less the tax deductibility, of contributions to professional
associations or other organizations lobbying for desirable legislation.

Apparently the search for ways to avoid federal and state taxes
led legions of businessmen in the 1950s to establish their own
foundations that would later be categorized as hip-deep in "self-
dealing" with respect to loans and property leases between the
firm and members of the owning family. Equally troubling to

Congress were the stockpiling and freezing of business assets and controlling blocks of common stock in the coffers of inert private foundations that would never have to pay income or inheritance taxes or make charitable contributions. The remedy in the 1969 act was to mandate that each private foundation make reasonable annual cash disbursements (ultimately amounting to at least 6 percent of the market value of the assets held) even if it meant invading the foundation's capital.

The 1969 act changed the metabolism of thousands of hitherto hibernating foundations and, with its new rules and definitions as to what constituted appropriate activities for such foundations, made trustees take exquisite care to maintain the taxexempt status of the funding agency and to make sure that grantees were qualified as recipients. As Reverend Coffin notes, foundation executives, in fear that the IRS will take away their tax-exempt status, refuse to admit that they are political, but "What that really means is that we don't want to get into leftist politics. It won't hurt us to be called conservatives."[3] The DJB trustees had the kind of honesty that Coffin was looking for and, describing the way that D. J. Bernstein used his personal nontax-deductible funds in tandem with his foundation's tax-exempt funds, they wrote as follows in their final report.

We decided not to jeopardize DJB's several million dollars by grants that could be challenged by tax authorities, ever on the alert for non-orthodoxy. We recognized that we would be on uncertain ground in helping dissenters and those challenging official injustice and indifference. Hence we sometimes moved through the approved channels of public foundations (DJB is a "private" foundation). This explains the frequent appearance in the detailed report of such bold and efficient public foundations as the Regional Young Adult Project, the American Civil Liberties Foundation, and the Youth Project.[4]

The avowed objective of progressive social change philanthropists is still to help disadvantaged groups to make major, enduring improvements in their status in our society. Achieving social justice and distributive equity ordinarily requires significant changes in our system, and such changes in turn require political activity and responsive legislatures. Successful political activity is inherently an important goal for the many section

501(c)(3) "educational" grantee corporations that are affiliated with section 501(c)(4) "lobbying" groups and even PACs (political action committees). Many funders, as individuals, make nondeductible contributions to section 501(c)(4) groups and PACs, together with deductible grants to section 4945f organizations for regional voter registration programs. Keeping these activities sufficiently separate in order to satisfy the Internal Revenue Service is a constant concern, as the next section's review of the recent history of funders' attempts to invigorate the political process demonstrates.[5]

The Political Question in Recent Decades

Political action in the United States is packaged in several ways of interest to the social change community. Which set of activities and how much of them constitute unacceptable political behavior on the part of tax-exempt organizations in the eyes of the IRS is of equal interest, but despite, or in spite of, the IRS's silent presence, social change remains unthinkable without some political muscle to effect change.

The mild-strength potion of political remedies concocted by social-changers comes in the form of books and lectures prepared by the denizens of think tanks for the education of the general public, together with discreet presentations to policymakers, notably legislators and their staffs.

A slightly stronger potion is generated by educational organizations asking their members to write their elected executives and legislators about a given issue. The growth during the 1970s in the use of the automatic mailing machine attached to a computer dramatically changed this aspect of politicking. No household in the United States escapes the deluge of "junk mail" sent out by both established and ad hoc organizations on the right and the left, some of which is overtly related to electoral campaigns but framed as education about a topical issue.

Grass-roots organizing to empower citizens also has political implications at all levels of the federal system. Examples of national groups that have obtained political power as a result of organizing and sending mountains of mail are the National Rifle Association, some of the environmentalist groups, and recently the American Association of Retired Persons. It is harder to find examples of statewide coalitions of grass-roots organizations able to influence their state legislatures; the Montana Alliance for Progressive Politics is one. A strong but often evanescent potion is the demonstration, sometimes with quiet picketing, at other times with sufficient fervor on the part of participants and the authorities that skulls are cracked, civil rights are jeopardized, and media "photo opportunities" are created.

The potions with the strongest and most lasting effect are administered by the voters themselves at the ballot box, "turning the rascals out" as a result of a direct political campaigning. The problem is that not enough people vote, and so the social-changers on all sides of the political spectrum began to develop strategies for getting their supporters to the voting booth. The civil rights movement that flowered in the late 1950s and, after years of turmoil, produced the political climate that made passage of the Civil Rights Act of 1964 feasible, was centered on making it possible for Southern blacks to register to vote.[6] Implementing that legislation by removing state and local barriers to registration and inducing citizens to register and then vote has turned out to be a continuing challenge, not only for blacks but for Hispanics across the nation. Voter registration and GOTV (get out the vote) campaigns remain strong contenders for support from progressive social change funding organizations.

The presidential election of 1980 took the progressive social change movement by surprise. They could not accept the idea that Ronald Reagan had a true mandate, since his 43.9 million votes represented only 27.8 percent of the votes that theoretically could have been cast. Unfortunately, only 53.9 percent of the voting-age population had gone to the polls that year, and so the race was on to register the unregistered and redress the balance in 1984.

The progressive social change community, together with unions and some churches, sponsored many voter registration drives in the 1982, 1984, and 1986 elections, and another book not yet written is the history of the Citizens' Action movement based on the hope for consolidated voting by members of progressive grass-roots organizations in the several states. Groups to the right of Reagan, especially those representing religious fundamentalists, were also active in GOTV campaigns. One of the major progressive strategies was to mount such drives in neighborhoods and other places, such as welfare offices, where poor and minority populations (of the sort being most affected by Reagan's program cutbacks) were to be found. The results were generally disappointing, partly because many who did get registered did not actually vote, partly because not all the new registrants voted the "right way."

For the 1988 campaign, a new strategy to supplement plain voter registration drives was developed by such new organizations as USA VOTES and the Forum Institute. Both groups intend to increase citizen participation in the United States, which currently has the lowest rate of voter turnout among all industrial democracies in the world. As Forum (established in 1981) wrote prior to the 1988 election:

Forum's goal is to reinvigorate democracy and the belief that every vote counts. The decline in voter participation is not a simple academic issue, but rather a fundamental test of American governance. With fewer and fewer people participating, we risk a deepening paralysis in the ability of state, local, and national leaders to build consensus for the resolution of the pressing social and economic problems that plague our communities, nation and planet. . . .

Our strategy is centered on support for nonpartisan, grassroots organizations which are capable of bringing low-income and minority people into America's democratic process. . . .

Forum makes grants to local, state, and national organizations which register, educate and motivate voters who traditionally have had the lowest rates of political participation and representation—primarily low-income and minority people. In addition, Forum makes grants to organizations which conduct non-partisan issue education so as to make people aware of their stakes in the political process and create a more informed electorate. We also support reform efforts, media and research projects to overcome the structural and attitudinal barriers to a more participatory democracy.[7]

Working with the Funders Committee on Voter Registration and Education, the Norman Foundation, the Youth Project, and the Citizen Participation Project, and with Frank Smith and John Richards as consultants, Forum and the Youth Project identified states where grants would be made to GOTV organizations. In the fifteen states selected, forty million people did not vote in 1984, and of that total 25 percent were not even registered to vote and the remaining were not motivated to do so.

Forum constituted itself as a vehicle for donors who are not able to investigate individual groups and took responsibility for ferreting out accurate information in order to make informed decisions about who can use grants most effectively and for following up to make sure that the grants were used well. Forum's criteria for selecting grantees included:

—Organizations working on issues of unquestionable public value as identified by low and moderate income constituencies, historically under-represented minorities, and others representing socially important concerns. These efforts are evaluated in the context of the state's indigenous political economy and the potential to excite broad-based voter participation.

—Organizations with a well-defined constituency and geographic base targeted to communities of nonvoters and infrequent voters. Again, priority is given to those working among historically under-represented populations such as blacks, hispanics, women, and the working and unemployed poor.

—Organizations with an effective strategy and demonstrated ability to target, educate and mobilize a meaningful block of citizens. In evaluating such capability, we consider the provision of technical and financial assistance to help further a group's ability to structure, staff, and organize their programs in the most effective way. We also provide legal and technical assistance to local projects to assist them in understanding the federal tax and election laws which govern nonpartisan registration, education, and get-out-the-vote programs.

—Organizations which are capable of holding elected officials accountable to the concerns of their constituents and, thereby, demonstrate the value in voting. The ability to develop leaders, raise funds from members, and work in coalition with allies are also strong indicators of an organization's sophistication and credibility in a community, and therefore qualities considered in our funding decisions.[8]

By the end of the 1988 campaign, the Forum Institute (with its 157 donors and "such dedicated champions as Senator Alan Cranston") reported that it granted $2.2 million to more than 50 community-based projects that registered over a million voters.

Table 11.1
Distribution of GOTV Funds, 1988 Campaign

Nature of activity	Amount allocated (in millions)	Percent of total raised
Local and state programs	$ 8.5	71 %
National groups	2.5	21
Administration, monitoring and fundraising	1.0	8

Rob Stein and Joy Jacobson of the USA VOTES Committee estimated its efforts resulted in over $12 million being contributed
to support similar nonpartisan voter participation programs in
1987–1988. These funds supported a wide range of educational,
registration, and get-out-the-vote activities of more than 50
groups in the 18 states, as well as administration, training, and
back-up support services of national organizations. Table 11.1
is their approximation of how funds were allocated.

USA VOTES also reported that these funds were contributed
by over 300 individuals, corporations, unions, and foundations.
Approximately 63 percent of the financial support (about $7.5
million) was provided by individual donors and family foundations; 25 percent (or $3 million) by large private foundations;
and 12 percent (about $1.5 million) by unions and corporations.

In addition to linking information on such issues of importance
to the community as the environment, problems of seniors, jobs,
transportation, and education to voting, USA VOTES reported
that most of the designated nonpartisan groups also conducted
intensive get-out-the-vote campaigns with door-to-door canvass
operations, phone banks, leaflets, and transportation on election
day. Some 500 copies of two different legal manuals—one commissioned by the Youth Project and the other by the Funders
Committee on Voter Participation—were distributed to community-based groups as aids in training local organizers and
volunteers on how to conduct nonpartisan voter programs. The
accomplishments of USA VOTES were summarized as follows:

—Significant reform of voter registration laws moved forward in Congress with support from bipartisan group of fifty-seven U.S. Representatives and five U.S. Senators. More than 160 national groups have endorsed the legislation. We expect the legislation to be reintroduced early 1989 and to move rapidly forward with broad bi-partisan support.

—Approximately 300 individuals, foundations, corporations and unions contributed in excess of $12 million to a wide range of nonpartisan efforts to help expand voter participation in America.

—Funds USA VOTES helped to raise supported non-partisan civic, public interest, human service and civil rights groups nationally and in 18 states.

—Collectively, the groups devoted 33 percent of their resources to voter education and get-out-the-vote activities and 67 percent to voter registration.

—These groups registered a total of 1.1 million citizens in key states and encouraged 1.5 million new registrants and occasional voters to vote on November 8th.[9]

There is clearly a good deal of overlap between the USA VOTES and the Forum Institute's reckoning. In any case, after the election, Forum wrote:

While the million voters registered by Forum's grantees is a small percentage of all Americans who were eligible to vote in 1988, a million new registrations represent a significant accomplishment and are very important to the electoral process. For example, a shift of about half that amount, or 522,000 votes, in nine states, would have changed the result in the electoral college.

State figures also show that Forum activities made a significant contribution to voter turn-out. In New Jersey, where the U.S. Senate race was decided by a margin of eight percent, the groups funded by The Forum Institute registered two percent of the state's voters. In a small state such as Nevada, the experience of a few thousand voters can help overcome the cynical view that "my vote doesn't make a difference"; there the margin of victory in the U.S. Senate contest was only 14,000 voters, approximately the number targeted by The Forum's grantee for its nonpartisan get-out-the-vote drive.

Despite the clear significance of small blocks of voters and the importance of every vote, half of all eligible voters—90 million Americans—did not vote in this election, marking the lowest turnout in 64 years. Consequently, George Bush was elected with the support of just 27 percent of the electorate, which is the lowest percentage to elect an American president in this century.[10]

The progressive social change community was taking stock of its situation as I began to write this book. That there had been gains as well as disappointments from the effort to turn out voters was some solace, but no one doubted that the effort would continue. Some thoughts about where the political energies of the progressive social change movement may go in the 1990s are presented in the following chapter.

People and Prospects for the 1990s

Lessons from the 1988 Election

Broad citizen participation at all levels of the deomcracy represents the critical difference between pluralists, populists, progressives and those they struggle against—plutocrats, autocrats,
and worse, fascists and fundamentalists. Yet 1988 saw a president elected by a mere 27 percent of the electorate. What did
that say about the effort over several decades to build a progressive citizen action movement or coalition? What did that say
about the efforts of progressive social change philanthropists to
fund community organizations that would inspire sympathetic
voters to exercise their franchise?

After the election, the Forum Institute wrote its supporters
that

more than ever, we all have a profound responsibility to understand
the multiple and complex reasons for mounting voter disaffection and
to address the erosion of democratic participation in the United States.
. . . We want to know how voter participation in [our] areas compared
to the general trend, which strategies worked best, and what were the
attitudinal, political, and organizational obstacles to systematic efforts
to increase voting.[1]

In the weeks after the election, groups of leading progressives met to begin evaluating the past and preparing for the future. One group was convened in New York City by Frank Riessman of the *Social Policy* journal, the other meeting was organized in Boston by Harriet Barlow of Common Practice and the Blue Mountain Center, who later distributed copies of critiques of the sessions written by Don Hazen of *Mother Jones* magazine and S. M. Miller of the Commonwealth Institute and professor of sociology at Boston University. Hazen describes attendance at the Boston meeting:

The group (though mostly white) represented most major issues and constituencies currently actively working on progressive issues in the U.S. Leaders were in attendance from the toxics, save the family farm, peace, environmental, labor, housing movements and organizations including: Jobs with Peace, Center for Third World Organizing, the National Toxics Campaign, the Public Media Center, the Rainbow Coalition, Acorn, Greenpeace, Nuclear Times, Farm Aid, Labor Institute, Mother Jones, Mobilization for Survival, etc. were represented. The group of some 60 people ranged from self conscious leftists working for "deep, profound lasting change," to issue reformers and pragmatic progressives deeply involved in electoral politics.[2]

Obviously much of the talk, as reported by Hazen, was about the problematic future of a Democratic party "increasingly dominated by corporate interests" and the feeling that "the prospects of a viable progressive candidate being nominated and elected seem remote." The importance of these meetings for this book are the thoughts expressed about the progressive movement as the foundation for electoral gains, but reference must be made to the widespread concern across the whole political spectrum about the cost of campaigns, more specifically the cost of television time. Hazen continued:

As we gathered in Boston to discuss the state of affairs, we had to face a rather sobering reality: the double whammy of the gross influence of money on politics and increasing failure of the media to provide a check on the deterioration of democracy. More and more, American policy and public opinion is shaped by large amounts of money and media manipulation. Standard forms of organizing and communicating need to be reassessed; funding patterns reexamined to see if money is not being poured into a deep black hole. . . . While the media becomes increasingly monopolized, the media fare becomes more sanitized. The audience becomes more passive, less and less capable of critical thinking, or more and more cynical about any prospect of change. Thus, the election of 1988 breaks new records for low levels of voter participation. "Why bother" many citizens are continuing to say.[3]

Nevertheless, citizens are active in their communities. I was never quite clear about the "thousand points of light" that candidate George Bush talked about during the campaign (but see the chapter note for some postinauguration definitions).[4] Probably he was referring to the volunteers that President Reagan hoped would fill in the gaps in social services caused by cutbacks in federal programs. While Bush did once mention Willie Velasquez, who was a long-time member of the Youth Project's board of directors and whose Southwest Voter Registration Education Project had received funds from progressive social change foundations, I assume that most of the grantees mentioned in this book were beyond his ken at the time. In any case, what S. M. Miller called "a laundry list" of movements and causes exists, and Hazen, noting that there is no "interconnected movement," reported that the conferees found the family farm movement in fair shape, the peace movement struggling, and groups such as ACORN and the Center for Third World Organizing making progress. In this context, a few of Hazen's further comments are worth repeating here.

No question about it, it's increasingly difficult to find inspiration for social change work. It seemed clear that movement politics is at a nadir, as Leslie Cagen put it: "Why is the movement? Who are we? There is no coherent we." However, among the group gathered at Tufts, were a number of virtually life-long organizers, many individuals toughened by years of frustration and almost impossible obstacles. And despite the dark clouds, there were plenty of expressions of hope and outlines of plans and strategies.

In fact, if there was a theme for the future in the room, it was getting back to basics, and digging in for the long haul. Person after person, while admitting that little has worked successfully during this era of Reagan/Bush, advocated putting more emphasis on long term planning and less on short term gain, like investing a lot of time and resources in a particular election. Political education, building new cadres, developing curriculum for younger organizers, looking back at history to avoid future mistakes, were all tactics given emphasis. . . .

A second convergence of opinion seemed to emerge around a growing sense of linkage around the production excesses of profit driven corporate multinationals. The goal would be a movement towards stopping polluters and poisoners at the source, and community control of resources aimed at stopping destruction of the earth and its resources. The linkage of the toxics, farm, peace, environment, and social justice movements is obvious when the targets are the arms producers, the chemical producers, the tree cutters, the gentrifiers, agribusiness and the economic system that underwrites their activities including the World Bank, IMF, and the U.S. Government.[5]

S. M. Miller, a sociologist and also a member of the Field Foundation's board, supplied a more profound critique of the proceedings. His comments reflected his own low opinion of the "laundry list" approach and his feeling that progressives had not demonstrated their ability to focus their efforts, to organize coalitions among themselves, or to capitalize on positive and moral sentiments among the American people. While he recognized the intrinsic validity of the various items that were on the progressive agenda, he wrote:

Progressives may have problems of ideological leakage and organizational linkage, but there is out there a sense among ordinary Americans that fundamental change is occurring in the United States and its world position. Even if a major recession, which might open the way to deep progressive action (or to further reaction!) does not occur, progressive opportunities should grow in the next years. Organizing at the grass roots is crucial. But I thought that people in Boston were saying that it is not enough; "political education" became the codeword for the effort to move more broadly and deeply. At this point, this call for political-ideological-theoretical education is a sentiment rather than a direction. . . .

The Boston group had its fascination—with political education, particularly of "cadre," a word of undoubtedly deep significance to rank-and-file members. . . . [However,] local leaders and rank-and-filers do not understand the broader significance of what they are engaged in and the links to and necessity of profound economic and social change.

Is limited outlook of members and local leaders due to neglect and difficulty of deploying resources to political education or is it a by-product of the uncertainties of progressive leaders? If the ruling class is in ideological disarray, it was said, so is the progressive world. For example, what kind of "anti-corporation" outlook do we share?

Since members join and engage in actions on specific issues, largely unaware of the broader and more profound agenda of those who re-cruited them, there is a disjuncture at an early point. Activists do not see a movement, they see an injury or injustice that should be rectified. As was said in Boston, they do not recognize "the movement" made up of the diverse organizations that make up the progressive world and somewhat sharing a world-view.

My reaction is that "political education" is another escape from critical evaluation of progressive activities. If we want to consider enlarging political education, the first question should be: Why have we done so badly at it so far? The answers lie not primarily in time, methodology or pedagogical technique but in ideological uncertainties and classes and in the very nature of organizing approaches.

Progressives have shown in the '70's that organizing can be done in almost any community on almost any issue. That has been a heroic achievement. (It would be well worth examining why organizing has been so possible: is it the approach? the times?) The assumption is that this type of organizing can move from fairly specific interest concerns to a deep and broad ideological shaping, operating effectively with stability and perhaps expanding in scale. If this assumption is largely valid, then political education might proceed with relative ease. If not—trouble.[6]

Trouble, self-doubt, fear, denial, and cynicism characterized the American political scene as reported by Hazen and Miller in their separate ways, with progressives hardly better off than middle-of-the-roaders and right-wingers. The way to the goal of getting a liberal-to-progressive administration seems to be blocked for the near term. Fortunately, the fortunes of organi-zations formed to fight for pollution control or arms control or welfare reform are not tied to any political party, nor are the opportunities open to progressive social change philanthropists for helping empower poor and minority groups restricted by the ability of the Democratic party to reorganize itself after the 1988 debacle.

The years will roll by. The participating grantees and funders at the New York and Boston postelection meetings will have gone back to their social change occupations and will remain part of the informal network about which this book has been written. Whether they also return to basic organizing, whether they are able to form useful and viable coalitions for the 1990s, and whether they will be able to do a better job of reaching the hearts and minds of more Americans than they were able to do in the past only time will tell, but in the following final section I try to outline the trends that the writing of this book suggests will be central to their tasks.

Strategizing for the Future

The quest for empowerment of low-income and minority people is, by definition, the central theme for progressive social change philanthropists. The think tanks and get-out-the-vote campaigns that are funded by those philanthropists are only means to the end of helping grass-roots groups become viable actors at the state and local level.

No one needed to dwell on this central theme of empowerment as the basic justification for social change activism in the deliberations at the post–1988-election gatherings of social-changers, which found the progressive movement lacking interconnectedness and the national political scene in disarray. Such tacit acknowledgment that all the attendees were involved in the quest is testimony to the effectiveness of a quarter-century's work.

That work includes the elevation of the Campaign for Human Development as a permanent activity for the United States Catholic Conference. It is manifest in the address by Reverend William Coffin I quoted in Chapter 5. The quest, in effect, has been resanctified as part of our common morality.

The need for empowerment, moreover, has never been greater. The gap between rich and poor is growing, and economists are now showing that such income disparities will be more exacerbated by the recession that is threatened in the near future than was seen in past recessions.[7] Moreover, the United States seems to have developed an underclass of functionally illiterate and often drug-impacted individuals who are as much the victims of our present system as they are the agents of their own destruction.

Eliminating the causes that create such an underclass is a burden to be shared by conservatives and progressives. So too is the need to protect the U.S. Constitution and the Bill of Rights for all Americans and to make such rights operational for Native Americans, immigrants, women, and minorities generally. These needs have generated many of the issue-based causes and activist community organizations that have been supported by the progressive social change funders.

CHD's criteria specify that the community organization to be funded must "benefit a poverty group" and "members of the poverty group must have the dominant voice in the project." In short, the work is to be done *by* those being empowered rather than *for* them as is characteristic of most charitable services and grants to think tanks. I find no evidence that the generic nature of grass-roots organizing has changed over the past few decades since the late 1960s when, in the words of the Youth Project, "literally thousands" of citizen-based organizations sprang into being, nor do I find evidence that it will change.

A major problem to be faced in the quest for empowerment, however, is the relative lack of trained organizers to help get the process started and to help steer the new organization there-after. Empowerment requires more quiet determination than angry demonstrations, and organizers accomplish more by per-suasion than by anger, as Nancy Taylor pointed out in a recent speech to a group of professional organizers.[8] And, as Coffin noted, trained organizers probably know more about how to operate than a neophyte local activist does, regardless of the particular issue that spurs the organizing effort.

Issues change from time to time, with yesterday's issue on center stage giving way to today's, but the supply of trained organizers is threatened by inadequate salaries and benefits. Mike Clark's survey (quoted in Chapter 10) suggested some remedies to maintain and increase the supply of experienced organizers. Progressive social change funders will undoubtedly be asked in the future as in the past to support a variety of training institutes and workshops and a variety of methods, including better salaries and adequate health insurance, for enhancing the economic security of those who are devoting their life to the job of organizing.

A number of training institutes exist, such as the Highlander School, the Midwest Academy, and the Northern Rockies Action Group. More may be formed in the future. Undoubtedly, more research as to what constitutes effective organizing in different circumstances and around different issues needs to be done to improve the training offered, but this brings us back to David Hunter's conclusion that "Foundations should self-consciously and explicitly support serious work by people, organizations and institutions undertaking radical research and design" that will do some "heavy thinking not restricted by conventional models, not restrained by taboos, not governed exclusively by the guidelines of the 'art of the possible' " if the progressive social change community is "to make headway toward the fundamental changes all those people are talking about."[9] So funders in the future will not lack for proposals from think tanks and other intermediate groups. Hazen reported that some people at the postelection conferences advocated the establishment of a public interest academy. The staff members of think tanks and training institutes, as well as progressive public servants and elected officials, however, will have had their own basic training in the nation's colleges and universities, but only a handful of universities offer coursework that is relevant to a career as a community organizer. Moreover, only a relatively small number of professors are engaged in research that would help organizers in the field or that helps the process of "thinking globally but acting locally," and only a handful of university presidents are calling for a rededication of their students to the ideals of public service, as President Bok at Harvard did in his 1988 commencement address. Bok also noted the dangerous disparity between salaries in the public and private sectors, a disparity that is even greater at the local level.

Not much mention was made at the postelection meetings in New York and Boston about the status of the funding arm of whatever progressive movements exist. The demands upon funders for support of the various programs that would be helpful in sustaining and reinvigorating progressive programs could escalate year by year through the 1990s. My rough estimate (in

Chapter 3) was that total funds from progressive foundations, individuals, and churches are currently about $100 million. Practically everyone in the progressive social change community is painfully aware of the termination of the Stern Fund, the Field Foundation, and other stalwart supporters that were active in the past. David Hunter, something of a professional optimist, declared in his speech to the National Network of Grantmakers, however, "It's hard for me to believe that there isn't some new money out there to take their place. . . . "

But that new money will come primarily from a new generation of donors. The Yale study concluded that fewer large endowments on the lines of the original Rockefeller, Ford, Sage, and, later, MacArthur Foundations can be expected in the future, partly because there are so many newer alternative ways of giving away money and partly because there are so many more qualified recipients than had existed in earlier times and under different tax laws. No one has speculated on the willingness of the new stock market and high-technology billionaires to fund progressive social change activities, even to the extent that Ford and some of the other older foundations do in supporting academic research, national policy institutes, selected public-interest educational campaigns, and occasional investments in or loans to local community economic development programs. Only a few corporate or community foundations indicate interest in funding social change grantees.

Mike Clark pointed to the "greying" of the generation of 1960s activists and community organizers, and an equivalent greying is taking place of the generation of young wealthy individuals mentioned in the Yale and Schervish-Herman studies cited in Chapter 2. Most of the donor-members of the new breed of public charitable foundations, some assembled under the banner of the Funding Exchange but many operating independently as part of an informal network, are currently in their late thirties or early forties. Just as fund-raising has become a fine art for all charitable, academic, and social change grantees, annual fund-raising by these public foundations is of primary concern, but their attempts to attract new donors over fifty or not yet thirty years of age have not been noticeably successful in recent years.[10] David Hunter may be correct about the size of the pool of prospective donors to progressive social change foundations, but creating a new generation of donors among the young, self-made wealthy as well as inheritors of sizable fortunes, represents a major challenge for the field. Some encouragement stems from the growth of funding groups organized by and for women. The 1990s, however, will be a testing period as to whether the nation can woo its citizens away from excessive hedonism and materialism toward greater social investment in education, health, and the general welfare. It will also be a time for discovering whether a whole new class of donors, large and small, can be induced to support progressive social change activities.

In my first chapter, I wrote that the philanthropic system in the United States is itself a set of networks that is a part of our whole social system, a part of our political economy and that the progressive social change philanthropists are a miniscule part of the system by which Americans support their nongovernmental nonprofit institutions. A host of well-advertised megatrends are affecting American society, and their impact on the prospects of the progressive end of the spectrum will be no different than on the conservative side.

For the nation as a whole, getting new donors for the usual run of charitable and educational institutions is just as important as getting new donors interested in helping empower the poor and minority populations. Civil and economic rights are as important to "yuppies" and fundamentalists as to members of various disadvantaged groups. Strengthening our fragile national economy by such steps as reducing military expenditures and providing health insurance for all citizens (especially children) is just as much a national imperative as improving labor-management systems and encouraging cooperative worker-owned enterprises.

We live in the information age, and intelligent dissemination of critical thinking is one of the greatest challenges facing our society. We may or may not need better computers, but we clearly need better methods of informing kids in schools and colleges—and their elders—about the moral imperatives of an equitable society, in addition to giving them a more profound sense of history and the other intellectual tools they need. We clearly need better ways of educating citizens about their political choices, freeing ourselves and our legislators from the present system by which elections are dominated by the financial demands of the media.

The need for better schooling and information is matched by the nation's need for broader citizen education. My sense is that the survival and growth of the networks of progressive social change funders and grantees depend upon the same kind of improvements in the flow of critical information about issues and causes that are required to raise the level and breadth of public debate in the nation as a whole.

The lesson of this final chapter is that the progressive social change community has a great deal of mutual self-education and development of strategies in store for itself over the 1990s. Existing funders are being urged to develop closer ties among themselves and to bring their more traditional peers into the field. Grantees are being asked to provide better demonstrations of their managerial capacities and their abilities to work with one another. Both donors and donees face the task of educating the Internal Revenue Service, the general public, and legions of prospective donors, that economic and political empowerment are not only indistinguishable warps and woofs of the social fabric but are socially acceptable objects for philanthropy.

Appendix: Analysis of Prototypical Project Grants

Introduction

In the course of writing this book, I discovered that many people had very little knowledge of the kinds of grants that are made by progressive social change funders. Perhaps this is not surprising in a society where so many citizens have so many ways to isolate themselves from less fortunate members of their communities and to avoid involvement with organizations intent upon effecting progressive social change.

I have prepared this appendix with its set of 91 descriptions of actual grants carefully selected to illustrate the various ways that grants can help empower different kinds of people. The grants were selected by analysis of the 1,482 items in my computerized database and are distributed by subject category as shown in the following table of contents.

Contents	Number of Cases
Grants for Community Organizing	9
Grants for Native American Organizations	
Tribal rights and identity	4
Native American women and health issues	1
Communications	1
Support for Native American economic progress	3

Grants for Black Organizations
Black community organizing   3
Black civil rights projects   2
Economic progress for blacks   3
Enterprise development for blacks   5
The special role of ACORN projects   3
Housing and neighborhood projects for blacks   3
Black media and education projects   2
Grants for Hispanic Organizations
Organizing in Hispanic communities   2
Hispanic concerns about immigration and other laws   2
Organizing around Hispanic economic issues   4
Hispanic housing and neighborhood projects   2
Hispanic communications networks   2
Grants to Asian Groups   1
Grants to Improve the Economy of the South   3
Grants Concerning the Farm Crisis in America   4
Grants Concerning National Economic Revitalization
Reindustrialization and labor studies   6
Women's economic status   2
Other Grants for Housing and Community Development   3
Grants Concerning Environmental Quality   5
Some Grants Concerning Health, Education, and Welfare   0
Other Grants Concerning Rights, Especially Women's   4
Topical Grants for Voter Registration Drives   4
Grants Concerning Peace and National Security
Topical grants on Central American issues   1
On other peace and national security issues   1
Other Media Projects   3
Grants to Help Build the Social Change Movement   3

The grant descriptions in this appendix have been excerpted from
the funders' annual reports. The funders are identified by their initials
in brackets following the quotation as follows: Campaign for Human

Development [CHD], Joint Foundation Support [JFS], Tides Foundation [TDS], Threshold Foundation [THR], and The Youth Project [TYP].

While some of the grants, especially to those working on a national scale, may not seem to meet the empowering criteria, almost all grantors look for a heightened capacity for community outreach, organizing, and administration on the part of their grantees as a further step toward autonomy.

The terse descriptions of grants in funders' annual reports provide a few hints as to why the grant was made and what the receiver will do with the funds but rarely reflect whatever difficulties of choice there may have been within the grantmaker's organization. They contain just enough information to enrapture, reassure, or even puzzle a reader unfamiliar with the field; my introductory comments at the start of each section may help.

Most of the vignettes that appear were written for the 1986 and 1987 annual reports issued by the Campaign for Human Development. CHD's write-ups are far more descriptive than the few that I selected from annual reports from the other five funding organizations in my sample and provide better identification regarding the race, sex, and economic status of the grantee's constituency.

Grants for Community Organizing

All of the community organizing projects listed here are empowering of the target populations. Many of these Campaign for Human Development grants involve collaboration between a number of parishes and mainline Protestant churches. Training of leaders and organizers is a constant theme, with the work of the Center for Third World Organizing exemplary in this respect.[1]

The grants in this section affect a diversity of disadvantaged groups in a particular locality. The techniques employed, however, are basically the same as those used for designated minority groups such as blacks, Native Americans, farmers, or low-income women.

NEW JERSEY CITIZEN ACTION
(New Brunswick, New Jersey)

Central Jersey Citizen Action, a chapter of New Jersey Citizen Action, is a two-county coalition of poor and working people's institutions organizing for social and economic justice. The goals of this chapter are to identify and develop local leadership among the poor, to involve large numbers of people in issue campaigns that can improve their quality of life, and to challenge the way the powerful public and private institutions operate without regard to community needs or justice. Central Jersey Citizen Action was started by a sponsoring committee in 1984. It has now grown to over twenty local organizations, including churches, senior citizens, Black and Hispanic, community and labor groups, and has a target of involving an additional thirty groups and seventy-five individual new members over the coming project year. The group has undertaken an extensive voter participation campaign in the county's poorest community, organized "early-warning" systems for protection of workers and the community against overnight plant closing, and launched a health care coalition and campaign to increase health care access for seniors and poor people. [CHD]

SALT LAKE CITIZENS' CONGRESS
(Salt Lake City, Utah)

The Salt Lake Citizens' Congress is made up of low-income people from the four poorest neighborhoods of Salt Lake City. Members come together to deal with common problems, such as housing availability, lack of adequate city services, job opportunities, utility rates, and toxics. Accomplishments include: securing $14 million in housing funds, protecting residential zoning, organizing strong neighborhood groups, and implementing telephone lifeline rates. This year the congress plans to implement a city jobs policy, develop alternative housing, reform utility assessments, prevent destruction of housing, increase city services in low-income neighborhoods, and control and clean up toxic waste. [CHD]

EL PASO INTERRELIGIOUS SPONSORING
COMMITTEE (El Paso, Texas)
Service and Voter Education Improvement Project

El Paso Interreligious Sponsoring Committee is a multi-issue coalition comprised of twenty church and civic groups working to improve services such as electricity, water, and sewage facilities in outlying areas of El Paso, Texas. The group is also conducting voter registration/education programs with assistance from the Southwest Voter Registration Education Project and has initiated a campaign to register and naturalize immigrants. [TYP]

IDAHO FAIR SHARE RESEARCH AND
EDUCATION FUND
(Coeur d'Alene, Idaho)
Silver Valley Organizing Project

The project goal is to develop a new community organization that will work with local church, labor, and senior groups to address economic and environmental issues in this mining region. [TYP]

MIDWEST UNEMPLOYED ORGANIZING PROJECT
(Milwaukee, Wisconsin)

The Midwest Unemployed Organizing Project will expand its unemployed organizations from four groups in Minnesota, Wisconsin, Illinois, and Iowa to groups in eight cities. Organizing will be concentrated in areas hit hard by unemployment, misery, and despair. The project envisions expanding to other Midwestern areas and eventually building a regional unemployed network. The organizing model is based on a three-year-old Milwaukee project, which annually produces over $2 million in benefits for its over 5,000 members. The union of unemployed negotiates directly with providers of goods and services for discounts or free benefits. The members also wage broader campaigns on issues concerning the poor, such as jobs, health care, and utility rates. The Midwest Unemployed Organizing Project empowers the unemployed, through cooperative action, to concretely improve their own lives. [CHD]

PORTLAND ORGANIZING PROJECT
(Portland, Oregon)

The Portland Organizing Project (POP) is a coalition of thirteen Protestant and Catholic churches that have joined together to build a broadbased community organization in Portland. Goals are to: (1) develop an organization that teaches low- and moderate-income people to act on problems that affect their communities; (2) convene a coalition of racially, ethnically, and religiously diverse groups to break down racism and stereotypes and to foster new relationships; (3) improve and strengthen member organizations through leadership training; and (4) bring about institutional change for low- and moderate-income people in Portland. POP has been successful in organizing a ban on fortified wine sales and eliminating disorderly conduct at a local convenience store. It also has won investigations and closures of neighborhood drug houses. [CHD]

VALLEY INTERFAITH
(Weslaco, Texas)

The Economic Revitalization of the Rio Grande project, sponsored by Valley Interfaith, addresses the problem of unemployment in the Rio Grande Valley by focusing on creating the conditions and removing the constraints that will allow for economic revitalization. This will be done by: (1) working with state officials to develop a food processing industry in the valley, (2) reorganizing unemployment compensation so that it fits the needs of the structurally unemployed of South Texas, (3) focusing on the expansion of successful small businesses in the valley, and (4) organizing workers' co-ops and other strategies that will involve building institutional relationships with financial and political leadership in the state on behalf of the structurally unemployed of South Texas. Valley Interfaith, a broad-based organization with a dues base of thirty-four parishes, serves a community of 600,000 in four counties across the river from Mexican cities and "colonias" totaling approximately 1 million people. The organization has built a strong record of accomplishments including: getting $125 million per year in new money to valley schools, obtaining $70 million with the passing of the Indigent Health Act of 1985, acquiring $2.5 million in developing funds for seven "colonias," stopping the burnings of PCBs in the Gulf of Mexico, and raising valley-wide voter registration from 150,000 to 248,000. Goals include attacking the structural unemployment of the poorest counties in the United States through development of relationships with new leaders of the valley and through establishment of a Texas-wide development bank along with other Industrial Areas Foundation organizations of Texas. [CHD]

GREATER BRIDGEPORT INTERFAITH ACTION
(Bridgeport, Connecticut)
Organizing Project

Greater Bridgeport Interfaith Action (GBIA) is a grass-roots, city-wide, interfaith coalition of ten congregations and one tenant association formed in 1984 to organize poor and working poor people to have a say in the decision-making processes affecting their lives. The purpose of GBIA's Organizing Project is to implement a congregationally based organizing model which will provide staff assistance to GBIA member groups, develop and train congregational and tenant leadership, provide a vehicle by which congregations can identify mutual concerns and work in coalition, and build a congregationally based citizen's organization capable of acting on Bridgeport's critical inner-city issues. GBIA has already organized the largest turnout ever in a tenant election and has won participation in redevelopment planning for a large public housing project slated for renewal. [CHD]

CENTER FOR THIRD WORLD ORGANIZING
(Oakland, California)
Minority Activist Apprenticeship Program

To meet the challenge of developing the talent pool of young minority activists into trained community organizers, the Center for Third World Organizing (CTWO) has instituted the Minority Activist Apprenticeship Program (MAAP). MAAP is designed to provide forty young minority activists with the opportunity to work for six weeks in direct action campaigns conducted by low-income minority organizations. After participating in a week-long organizer training session, trainees will be placed with five organizing projects in the Western United States. Following this six-week placement, trainees will complete another week of organizer training. CTWO is a network of Black, Latino, Native-American, and Asian activists and scholars who provide training, technical assistance, and issue analysis to over 200 organizations of low-income people of color. [CHD]

Grants for Native American Organizations

Tribal rights and identity

Strengthening cultural identities and restoring tribal rights are more important to Native American grantees than ordinary organizing programs. The Seventh Generation Fund, run by Native Americans, plays a special role in steering grants from the funding community to local groups. Land and fishing rights are especially important, and efforts in these areas have been supported by grants to such organizations as the Indian Justice Network, the Indian Law Resource Center, and the International Indian Treaty Council.

POTAWATOMI INDIAN NATION, INC.
(Dowagiac, Michigan)
The Road to Federal Recognition:
Education in Self-governance

State chartered in 1952, the Potawatomi Indian Nation Inc. provides administration and management support to the tribe, most of whom live in a four-county area in southwestern Michigan and a six-county area of northern Indiana. Activities in the Road to Federal Recognition: Education in Self-Governance project focus on three areas: (1) educating tribal members in the process and meaning of federal recognition, (2) developing a tribal judiciary system, and (3) assisting economic development within tribal communities. In the second year of this education and organizing process, the membership will begin to specify the role it wishes the tribe to play in the various legal systems. Also, the membership will begin to identify areas of economic and social development that should be given a priority and will form ad hoc working committees to provide specific guidance to the council and staff on programs and services to develop. [CHD]

SAN JUAN SOUTHERN PAIUTE TRIBE
(Tuba City, Arizona)

The Preservation of Tribal Lands project is an effort by the San Juan Southern Paiute Tribe to legally secure the traditional lands on which they have lived for hundreds of years. CHD funds will help pay for the expert witnesses necessary to successfully advance their case. Until this legal question concerning the Paiute's rights to their traditional lands is resolved, there is no assurance that the land will not be taken from them. It is impossible for the Paiutes to pursue economic development projects, given the uncertainty of the future of the land. The tribe has applied to the Bureau of Indian Affairs to become a federally recognized tribe; its application has been under active consideration for two years. Many of the tribe's members live a subsistence existence. This project will help them move toward increased self-sufficiency and security. [CHD]

YOUTH PROJECT/COLUMBIA RIVER DEFENSE
(Portland, Oregon)

The Youth Project/Columbia River Defense project provides legal support for the defense of seventy-five Native American people in fishing prosecutions in the United States, Oregon, and Washington courts. It is also appealing the eviction of Native American families living at "in lieu" fishing sites on the Columbia River. In addition to its litigation work, the project wants to ensure survival of traditional fishing communities and is working for the recognition of the continuing jurisdiction of the Mid-Columbia people's chiefs and councils. It seeks to organize the 400–600 native people living in the mid-Columbia region, enabling them to increase their input in decisions affecting fishing, hunting, gathering, housing, health, education, and the protection of burial and ceremonial sites. The project will create the framework necessary to enable the community to move toward self-government and community-controlled economic development. [CHD]

ANISHINABE AKEENG
(White Earth, Minnesota)

Anishinabe Akeeng is a land rights organization on White Earth Reservation concerned with reclamation of lands within the 1867 treaty area of the White Earth Anishinabe Indians (known as Chippewas). Less than 6 percent of the tribe's original land base is now under its control. The project's primary work has been in protecting the rights of Indian heirs to these lands through community education and empowerment; policy work—at the tribal, state, and federal level; opposition to land claims settlements; and, finally, litigation. It has conducted community meetings in each reservation village and has held a series of negotiations with the tribal council concerning land claims legislation, resulting in a long-term approach towards protecting land rights. [CHD]

Native American women and health issues

SEVENTH GENERATION FUND
(Forestville, California)
Native American Women Self-Help

The fund supports self-help efforts among Native American women in the Northwest. The grants were used to support the Northwest

Indian Women's Circle, whose goals include reestablishing traditional beliefs and values that help to strengthen the Indian family, developing economic self-sufficiency projects, and promoting leadership among Indian women. Two grants were received. [JFS]

Communications

LAKOTA COMMUNICATIONS, INC.
(Porcupine, South Dakota)
Lakota Nation Broadcasting Service

Founded in 1979, Lakota Communications is the South Dakota-based licensee of KILI Radio, this nation's first independently Indian-owned and operated radio station. The Lakota National Broadcasting Service will provide an Indian Radio Service to the Rosebud and Cheyenne River Reservations and to Rapid City, South Dakota. It will also develop Indian news and information for national distribution. The overall goal of the Lakota Nation Broadcasting Service is to provide the Lakota people with a consistent flow of information so that they can take control of their land base and the institutions that govern their lives. The major emphasis this year is a news and information collection system and development of a self-sufficiency plan to ensure that the project continues. [CHD]

Support for Native American economic progress

RURAL COALITION
(Washington, D.C.)
Native American Task Force

The Rural Coalition is a nine-year-old national alliance of some 130 member organizations dedicated to the development and implementation of public policies that benefit rural Americans, especially those who are poor or otherwise disadvantaged, and their communities. The Rural Coalition's Native American Task Force, organized in June 1986, will empower Native Americans across the United States to take more control of their health and lives. Work will focus on several issues: (1) environmental health on Indian lands, (2) chronic unemployment (often as high as 85 percent) in Indian Country, (3) continued threats of Indian land loss, and (4) the welfare of Indian children. The Task Force will activate a new network to improve federal Indian programs, organize campaigns on specific issues, research threats to Indian groundwater, and educate Indian and non-Indian rural organizations. [CHD]

IKWE MARKETING COLLECTIVE
(Osage, Minnesota)
Manomin Project

IKWE Marketing Collective is an economic development group working on the White Earth Indian reservation. It is concerned with development from a community-based perspective, centered on the skills and resources of the White Earth community. It believes that support of these traditions enables the community to reclaim its dignity, self-respect, and economy. The Manomin, or "wild rice," Project is aimed at reclaiming the community's rice crop and its value for sale and use. Rice leaves the reservation at a price of 65¢ a pound (green) with its resale value at $5–10 per pound. Collective members believe this money should stay in the community; project work is focused on marketing and infrastructure development. The project aims to build coalitions with other rice-producing native people. IKWE has successfully marketed crafts and rice at the retail and wholesale levels by mail order for two years. [CHD]

KALISPEL TRIBAL COMMUNITY
(Usk, Washington)
Kalispel Agricultural Development Project

The Kalispel Tribal Community, under the auspices of its tribal council, has initiated a variety of programs and activities that have as their purpose the continual maintenance of the health and welfare of its members. The Kalispel Tribe through its council has established an overall community economic development plan, which has as its central goal self-sufficiency. Part of that plan is to continue to develop and coordinate all agricultural projects under one enterprise structure. Current projects that are planned for expansion include a buffalo herd, leasing of grazing lands, and selling of hay and fruit tree orchards. New development plans call for irrigation projects and wild rice farming. [CHD]

Grants for Black Organizations

Black community organizing

A large portion of the CHD community-organizing grantees were categorized as black, black/Hispanic, or black/white groups in urban, rural/urban, and urban areas. The examples below are directed to black groups, including some directed to the welfare of black rural women.

HUMPHREYS COUNTY UNION FOR PROGRESS, INC.
(Belzoni, Mississippi)
Citizenship Empowerment

Through its Citizenship Empowerment project, Humphreys County Union for Progress (H-CUP) will develop a solid membership base to reflect a cross section of the black community of Humphreys County and give the organization a base from which to operate. It will provide ongoing leadership development training to H-CUP officials, staff, and community volunteers in an attempt to develop a pool of skilled persons to address membership and community needs and problems. Additional goals include further economic development in the county through the recruitment and establishment of business and industries in Humphreys County that will provide employment opportunities for blacks and other low-income persons with limited skills. [CHD]

OAKLAND COMMUNITY ORGANIZATIONS
(Oakland, California)
OCO: Building for Change

Oakland Community Organizations (OCO) is an organization that seeks to help people develop the power to effect changes within the institutions making decisions about their lives and that offers people the skills and opportunity to work in community with each other. Over the past year, OCO leadership and staff have charted a direction for the next ten years; OCO envisions an expansion of its constituency base that will result in an organization with the capacity to effect deeper systemic change. In the years ahead, OCO will revitalize and expand existing networks in OCO through four area teams (of fifteen to twenty leaders), increase the leadership and constituency base of OCO by establishing organizing committees in fifteen Oakland churches, and develop a strategy for the integration of neighborhood and church organizing efforts. [CHD]

HUNGER TASK FORCE OF MILWAUKEE
(Milwaukee, Wisconsin)
Network Empowerment Project

The goal of the Network Empowerment Project is to mobilize members of the Emergency Food Pantry Network as community leaders in the struggle for economic justice in Milwaukee's inner city. The project will build a multiracial, interfaith organization to fight for jobs and humane public assistance for low-income residents. The network is comprised of 100 food pantries, staffed by over 400 volunteers. The pantries serve over 25,000 people each month, 80 percent of whom are women and children. In 1987, the project goal is to expand leadership development efforts, mobilize public support for the job development strategy and involve female heads-of-household in public actions concerning welfare and job needs. [CHD]

Black civil rights projects

These projects cover grantees focusing on black civil and economic rights, including impediments to voter registration. Some of the other grants in my file were given to groups opposing the death penalty in Virginia and South Carolina.

CHRISTIC INSTITUTE–SOUTH
(Carrboro, North Carolina)

Christic Institute-South (CIS) is a small, public interest law firm that assists grass-roots groups in the South that are faced with false and politically motivated criminal charges intended to thwart their efforts to bring about change in their communities. CIS has successfully used the dual-faceted approach of a vigorous legal defense, combined with coalition-building and public education to defend grass-roots leaders and groups struggling for their own empowerment. Most but not all of CIS's work is in the area of racial justice. Through this defense and organizing, CIS seeks to free and strengthen grass-roots groups in their efforts to bring about effective change in the social, economic, and political life of their communities. [CHD]

KENTUCKY ALLIANCE AGAINST RACIST AND POLITICAL REPRESSION
(Louisville, Kentucky)
Developing a Community Network to
Combat Racist Practices

The Kentucky Alliance Against Racist and Political Repression is a local membership organization of both black and white activists with a track record of serving as a catalyst for community campaigns to combat racism. It has existed for eleven years and is recognized as the one framework in Louisville where black and white people concerned about social justice work together. It has developed successful campaigns against police brutality, Klan resurgence, racist violence, and discrimination in schools and employment. Objectives for 1987–1988 are to recruit, train, and activate at least 100 new volunteers and set up four additional task forces on: (1) the Klan and racist violence, (2) racism in police practices and the criminal justice system, (3) racism in schools, and (4) racism in employment practices. The goal of these task forces will be to educate the public, generate community campaigns, and change public policies. [CHD]

Economic progress for blacks

PEOPLE'S COALITION OF MISSOURI
(St. Louis, Missouri)
Economic Justice Project

The People's Coalition of Missouri (PCM) is a statewide alliance with both individual and organizational members. PCM began its work as a grass-roots effort to counteract proposed changes and cuts in federal programs for low-income and minority people. Over the last five years it has expanded its work to increase participation of low-income and minority persons in other public policy decisions affecting them and to change policies and practices that are misused and/or abusive. Major

PCM work has been in the areas of workfare, welfare, housing, employment, the federal budget, and criminal justice. The Economic Justice Project is a local outcome of PCM's work. Project objectives will focus on increasing participation in, and influencing the outcome of, public policy decisions and practices in the areas of jobs, income maintenance, and housing. [CHD]

BUILD

(Baltimore, Maryland)

BUILD Earner Association Organizing Project

The BUILD Earner Association Organizing Project is focused on the development of a means for unorganized low-wage workers to have a voice in the workplace as well as in their communities. Its goal is to organize within two years an association of low-wage workers that will begin negotiating on behalf of its members for better wages, benefits, and working conditions. BUILD is an interfaith, multiracial metropolitan citizens organization whose goal is to negotiate on behalf of Baltimore's poor and working class communities regarding the direction and development of Baltimore. BUILD has successfully led citizens' campaigns against both bank and insurance redlining, and recently negotiated the Commonwealth Agreement—a partnership among over 100 corporations, the Public School system, and BUILD aimed at upgrading the school systems and providing employment opportunities for high school graduates. [CHD]

WORKERS' RIGHTS ACTION PROJECT/ ASSOCIATION FOR THE RIGHTS OF CITIZENS

(New Orleans, Louisiana)

Workers' Rights Action Project

The Workers' Rights Action Project (WRAP) is an organization of low-income working and unemployed people, primarily low-wage service workers. Various issues that the organization focuses on include improved working conditions, adequate staffing, and just wages and benefits. WRAP strongly believes that when people are organized, believing in common goals, the unified body becomes powerful and effective. Currently there are twenty-six active workplace chapters. The organization's efforts have won hiring preferences for low-income workers in publicly funded projects, forced a company to establish the first ever pension fund for private-sector cafeteria workers in New Orleans, and helped community college workers win the battle to save their jobs from subcontracting. [CHD]

Enterprise development for blacks

A score of projects were designed to provide assistance to a wide variety of economic development projects, many of them organized as cooperatives. The examples that follow are typical of this kind of support.

FEDERATION OF SOUTHERN CO-OPS
(Epes, Alabama)
FSC Small Farmer Advocacy, Land Retention

Since 1971, the Federation of Southern Cooperatives has been involved in a program of cooperative economic development for 100 cooperatives and credit unions in the rural South. Over 25,000 low-income families are involved in the activities of these self-help groups. In 1984, the federation merged with the Emergency Land Fund to provide more services to small black farmers who were having serious financial problems and were in danger of losing their land. Through a program of advocacy for public policy changes, technical assistance and training for small farmers, and a cooperative development strategy, the federation is assisting low-income rural people to organize themselves for positive, progressive change. During two years of this program it has reached over 5,000 black landowners in eight states and assisted over 800 individual owners to save, retain and make useful over 35,000 acres of land, valued at over $10 million. [CHD]

FREEDOM QUILTING BEE
(Alberta, Alabama)

The Freedom Quilting Bee in Alberta, Alabama, is a handicraft producers cooperative. Forty women from Wilcox County, Alabama, are members. For the past five years, the Quilting Bee's sales have grown from $120,000 to $200,000. The average member receives $4,000 in wages from the co-op over an annual period. The co-op markets quilts, pot holders, table mats, pillows, and other handmade items. The project seeks funding to upgrade the management and marketing performance of the cooperative for future growth. [CHD]

BLUE DOT ENERGY WORKER CO-OP
(Junction City, Kansas)
Worker Owned/Worker Managed Cooperative

The Blue Dot Energy Worker Co-op is a minority worker-owned/worker-managed general construction business. The goal of the project is to form a competent general construction firm. Individual members have accomplished successful projects, such as renovation of a two-story limestone schoolhouse into a museum and construction of an 800-square-foot addition to a residential structure. At present, the co-op is weatherizing and rehabilitating 252 residential units for the Corps of Engineers; the contract is worth $150,000. It is also constructing a dual unit, 3,600-square-foot structure to house a training program for the disadvantaged; the contract value is $100,000. [CHD]

BLACKBELT HUMAN RESOURCE DEVELOPMENT CENTER
(Selma, Alabama)

MOM's Enterprises is a business venture organized to develop, manufacture, and market a line of cleaning products, beginning with a multipurpose cleaner called MOM's CleanAll. Since 1983 MOM's has been introducing the product in the Blackbelt region to school boards, churches, day-care centers, and other agencies. MOM's Enterprises was established to provide self-sufficiency for the MOM's organization. The Blackbelt Human Resource and Development Center (BBHRDC) is an organization devoted to promoting the quality of life of minority women and youth. MOM's Enterprises, the community economic development arm of BBHRDC, was initiated to start a manufacturing plant that will eventually produce an entire line of cleaning products. MOM's is an individual member organization with a membership of over 300, primarily in the Blackbelt region of Alabama. [CHD]

WARREN/CONNER DEVELOPMENT COALITION
(Detroit, Michigan)

Detroit East Community Development Corporation (DECDC) is a resident-controlled stock corporation with a one-shareholder/one-vote structure that will develop commercial real estate in the low-income communities on Detroit's east side. The goals of DECDC are job creation, commercial blight reduction, and community control. The Warren/Conner Development Coalition will manage DECDC for at least three years and hold a minority interest. Detroit East Community Development Corporation, as a separate development organization, will provide for the community the ability to do bricks-and-mortar development. The Warren/Conner Development Coalition, in operation since 1984 is a coalition of neighborhood councils, business associations, retail and industrial firms, institutions, and individual residents and workers. It works in four main areas: crime prevention, youth development, activism and advocacy, and community economic development. [CHD]

The special role of ACORN projects[2]

CHD favors members of the ACORN network. Grantees not listed here operate in New York, Pennsylvania, Arizona, Iowa, and Louisiana.

PINE BLUFF ACORN
(Pine Bluff, Arizona)
Pine Bluff Black Empowerment Project

Pine Bluff ACORN is a community organization of poor, primarily black, people that was founded in 1973 to advance the interests of low-income Pine Bluffians through empowerment of the low-income community. Pine Bluff ACORN campaigns saved the city bus system from extinction and expanded its service; brought Community Development Block Grant funds into the low-income black communities for sewer, water, natural gas lines, and home repair improvements; and won a major street improvement project in a low-income neighborhood. With the Pine Bluff Black Empowerment Project, ACORN will take advantage of the city council's new by-ward system to give the low-income, mostly black, half of the city a full share in the decision-making process of Pine Bluff. The project will focus on issues of city service and jobs along with intensive voter registration and get-out-the-vote campaigns and a leadership training program. [CHD]

ACORN
(Washington, D.C.)
ACORN Unemployed Council Organizing Project

Over the past three years, ACORN'S Unemployed Council Organizing Project (UCOP) has developed a model for organizing and empowering the long-term structurally unemployed and has built effective organizations of the unemployed in twelve cities. The UCOP plans to develop a new campaign to win job commitments, as well as financing commitments for job development projects, from major banks. Specific objectives for the UCOP are to build and strengthen Unemployed Councils in eight to twelve cities, to develop hiring halls that will strengthen and stabilize these Unemployed Councils by channeling jobs directly to the Unemployed Council members, to develop campaigns to win job commitments from banks, and to nationalize the campaign by targeting a major developer with projects in four to six ACORN cities with a nationally coordinated effort to win a company-wide hiring commitment. [CHD]

CHICAGO ACORN
(Chicago, Illinois)
Homesteaders Rights Project

The Homesteaders Rights Project is a campaign of Chicago ACORN to address the twofold problem of abandoned houses in low-income black Chicago neighborhoods and low-income black families who need housing. It helps the families organize to win title to the houses, prevent their demolition, rehabilitate them, and live in them. Since 1983 Chicago ACORN has grown to an organization of over 2,400 member families in seven neighborhoods around the city. Project goals include building the neighborhood organizations in the communities where homesteading is occurring and winning an expanded homesteading program. ACORN aims to: (1) speed up transfer of deeds, (2) develop a sweat equity model for rehab, and (3) win financing for the homesteaders for repair of the houses. [CHD]

Housing and neighborhood projects for blacks

The housing-related projects funded by CHD in black areas employ the full vocabulary of the field, from antidisplacement and tenant-rights issues, to urban homesteading and self-help construction projects. Notable as well are the direct investments in construction being made by CHD.

D.C. ACORN
(Washington, D.C.)
D.C. ACORN Public Housing Campaign

D.C. ACORN, established in 1983, is an individual membership project. It has a local membership of some 1,300 low- and moderate-income families. It has organized locally to win clean alleys, secure adequate street lighting, seal vacant properties, and increase police patrols. The ACORN Public Housing Campaign will reach out to organize and empower the 60,000 residents of the District of Columbia's public housing projects. The campaign envisions a membership of over 2,000 families from the housing projects in the next year. These members will advocate on their own behalf to win improvements in: (1) property maintenance, (2) tenant safety (fire, grounds conditions); and (3) tenant rights (rent mediation, displacement rights, and involvement in management). [CHD]

MARRERO TENANT ORGANIZATION
(Marrero, Louisiana)
"Developing Leaders—A Model Tenant Organization— Phase II"

The Marrero Tenant Organization is a public housing tenant group that has been able to establish control over all their management functions. It successfully promoted the employment of two qualified tenants; one is now the executive director and the other is the assistant. For more than fourteen years, tenants of the Jefferson Parish Housing Authority have struggled against insensitive managers, both black and white. Before the tenants got involved, maintenance was terrible and tenants were overcharged. But now, with tenants in control, there is progress. In 1986 the organization got $2.5 million to renovate housing units. Tenants are working on the remodeling projects; plans call for hiring at least fifty tenants. This project will develop written training materials, workshops, and direct actions that will assist other public housing tenants in the South. [CHD]

CALLAHAN NEIGHBORHOOD ASSOCIATION
(Orlando, Florida)
Anti-Displacement Organizing Project

The Callahan Neighborhood Project (CNA) will hire two organizers so that CNA can increase participation of neighborhood residents (especially renters) in the decision-making and actions necessary to change public policies that foster displacement and limit the availability of low-cost housing. Since 1977, CNA has redirected Community Development Block Grant funds to the neighborhood, resulting in paved streets, housing rehab programs, landbanking, and a recreation center. CNA members have worked with city officials to revise the zoning map and design a comprehensive neighborhood plan. [CHD]

Black media and education projects

AFFILIATED MEDIA FOUNDATION MOVEMENT
(New Orleans, Louisiana)
Media Organizing Project 1987

The Affiliated Media Foundation Movement (AMFM) is an association of poverty organizations and broadcast facilities committed to increasing the poverty community's access to and control of broadcast media outlets. Since 1977, AMFM has helped establish three radio stations, two in-progress television stations, and several cable programs directed and operated by low-income people. It recognizes the necessity of securing institutional change through ownership of media outlets. Through the Media Organizing Project, AMFM will assist groups in applying for twenty-five to forty new commercial FM frequencies. It will work with poverty organizations to (1) develop leadership, (2) recruit and train members and volunteers, and (3) construct and operate the stations to self-sufficiency. AMFM will establish a centralized production studio to support this network of low-income, community-based stations with high-quality relevant programming. [CHD]

WASHINGTON PARENT GROUP FUND
(Washington, D.C.)
Enrichment/Accountability

The Enrichment/Accountability project empowers low-income parents of public school children to identify educational deficiencies and target PTA enrichment funds to address them and to join parents city-wide working to improve public school funding and programs. The project helps parents become partners with administrators and teachers in setting school priorities. The project will (1) identify and obtain descriptive data on ten pilot schools, (2) organize the data to highlight educational problems in a school profile, and (3) use the school profiles to help parents advocate system-wide needs for programs. The group's advocacy has led the School Board to (1) add all day prekindergarten, (2) increase funds for texts and materials, (3) reduce class size, and (4) raise standards for teacher promotions. As a result of group pressure, the city council has added $72 million to the mayor's school budget since 1980. [CHD]

Grants for Hispanic Organizations

Organizing in Hispanic communities

Many of the dioceses in the CHD network serve Hispanic populations of many types, including Chicano and Puerto Rican, in both urban and rural settings across the nation. The grants are found in Northeast, Midwest, and Northwest communities as well as in Texas, California, and Florida. A representative selection of such grants to support organizing efforts follows.

COMMUNITIES ORGANIZED BY RURAL EFFORT
(Tucson, Arizona)

The emphasis of Communities Organized by Rural Efforts (C.O.B.R.E.) has been to organize rural communities. Through a training project that focuses on individual's rights as taxpayers and citizens, people have begun to feel empowered. This has resulted in physical improvements to the communities, including completion of a bridge and a food bank, still in operation. C.O.B.R.E. has participated in house-to-house voter registration. Its priority is to train and develop a broader leadership base to research and analyze problems and needs and to think through the necessary steps to bring about institutional change and attention. Strengthening and enhancing the informal network of the rural area has made the organization stronger. Issues that still need to be addressed include high utility rates, unchecked insecticide use, highest rate of prenatal deaths in the state, and inadequate drainage systems. [CHD]

THE MICHIGAN EMPOWERMENT PROJECT
(Grand Rapids, Michigan)
Hispanic Organizing Effort

The Kent County Hispanic Organizing Project is laying the groundwork for establishing a coalition organization. From its beginning in 1983, the group's purpose has been to build a base of power whereby Hispanics as a group can be self-directing and negotiate effectively in public decision-making. Activities have included a voter registration drive, culminating with a press conference at city hall; a public forum with city commissioners in 1985; a board of education candidate forum in 1986; parish development leadership training for a core group in 1986; and cooperative area-wide celebrations of Hispanic Heritage Week in 1985 and Hispanic Heritage Month in 1986. [CHD]

Hispanic concerns about immigration and other laws

The Hispanic communities have been deeply affected by recent furors over immigration laws, in addition to all the other legal problems faced by low-income and minority people. These grants provide examples of how CHD has used its funds to help improve such conditions.

INSTITUTO LABORAL DE LA RAZA
(San Francisco, California)

The Latino Labor Immigration Project will attempt to counteract two major setbacks for Latino workers in California: the passage of the Immigration Reform and Control Act of 1986 and the passage of Proposition 63—the "English only" initiative. The project goal is to lessen the negative impact of this legislation through a program of legal representation and employment rights education. Instituto Laboral, the sponsoring group, was founded five years ago by Latino workers who still direct the organization, with the purpose of providing urban Latino workers with a vehicle of their own for bringing about needed social change in the arenas of employment and labor. It has served over 10,000 workers through a program of leadership training, workers' rights education, and legal defense. [CHD]

MIGRANT ADVOCACY SERVICES, INC.
(Hereford, Texas)
Farmworkers' Rights Training and Advocacy Project

Field Sanitation, Workers' Compensation and Pesticides Migrant Advocacy Services Inc. was established in 1982 as a resource for migrant and seasonal farmworkers in Texas who seek to advance their social, economic, and political status through vigorous advocacy of their fundamental rights and concerns. The primary goal of the Farmworkers' Rights Training and Advocacy Project is to empower farmworkers with the skills and education necessary to bring about the institutional changes needed to improve their working conditions. The project will train farmworkers to utilize the institutional framework of newly passed field sanitation, workers' compensation, and pesticide statutes to end the vicious cycle of exploitation in the workplace. The project will employ and train three farmworker organizers who will "circuit ride" through the farmworker labor camps in the Texas Panhandle during the harvest season, educating workers to organize on their own behalf. [CHD]

Organizing around Hispanic economic issues

Grants to support Hispanics organizing around economic issues, especially in farming and fishing areas and in the garment industry, were made in Kansas, Ohio, Minnesota, and Oregon as well as in the more populous centers in Texas, California, and Florida.

HARVEST AMERICA CORPORATION
(Kansas City, Kansas)
Kansas Farmworker/Hispanic Political Project

The Kansas Farmworker/Hispanic Political Project will involve Harvest America Corporation in coalition with the Kansas Association of

Hispanic Organizations in order to work for specific institutional changes to improve life for farmworkers and rural, poor Hispanics in Kansas. Specifically, the project will address bilingual education, the drop-out problem of young Hispanics in Kansas schools, health care, and immigration. In previous years, Harvest America has developed Target Area Councils in four cities in Kansas. These councils have developed cohesion and the ability to work together to solve problems. [CHD]

GRANT COUNTY LOCAL OWNERSHIP
DEVELOPMENT CORPORATION
(Silver City, New Mexico)
Grant County Cooperative Venture Support

The Grant County Local Ownership Development Corporation is a community-based organization that seeks to emulate the success of the "Mondragon (Spain) Model" of production cooperatives. The aim of this project is to restructure the economic base of Grant County, New Mexico, so as to insure local ownership, control, and development through cooperative efforts by residents of the area. The goal of this project is to organize community groups and to prepare three of the groups to begin cooperative ventures. [CHD]

COMITE DE APOYO A LOS TRABAJADORES
AGRICOLA
(Kenneth Square, Pennsylvania)
CATA Pennsylvania Organizing Project

CATA is an organization of 2,000 workers in the fruit, vegetable, nursery, and packing house industries of New Jersey; the Pennsylvania mushroom industry; and the small coffee and citrus farms of Puerto Rico. Since 1979 it has brought workers together to gain decent, legal working and living conditions. CATA's work has included forming worker committees at dozens of locations to press for minimum wages, better housing, and protection from dangerous chemicals, as well as favorable unemployment and pesticide regulations. In 1986 CATA achieved an agreement improving housing and kitchen conditions at a local mushroom company. CATA is involved in interpreting the new immigration law to many of the 5,000–plus undocumented workers in the area. CATA aims to build membership and develop a leadership core among mushroom workers. [CHD]

LICEO SYLVAN
(El Paso, Texas)
Liceo Sylvan Sewing Co-op

"La Esperanza," the Liceo Sylvan Sewing Cooperative, is an economic development project. Through it, women of the border area in El Paso, Texas, work to assure family income while promoting self-dignity and community awareness. Members produce sewn items that promote Mexican values and have sold their merchandise to church groups, among others. Sales have increased noticeably because of new markets and improvement of quality. The co-op formed in 1982 and has continued to develop and grow since then. With development of expertise in marketing, the co-op should become profitable soon. [CHD]

Hispanic housing and neighborhood projects

NUEVA ESPERANZA, INC.
(Holyoke, Massachusetts)

Nueva Esperanza, Inc. is a community development corporation whose purpose is to address the negative policies and practices of city government officials and local investors toward the South Holyoke neighborhood. It has three goals: the delivery of affordable housing to families, the development of community leadership, and the delivery of supportive services for economic development. Through activities related to the successful rehabilitation of two eight-unit apartment buildings, Nueva Esperanza has brought about changes in the city's practice of selective code enforcement and arbitrary demolition. Also, the banking community has begun to make investments in the housing stock, reversing a fifteen-year pattern of redlining. Nueva Esperanza is a neighborhood-based organization that has been able to successfully coordinate the support and efforts of a variety of sectors: churches, state and federal government, local foundations, human service agencies, and other investors. [CHD]

COACHELLA VALLEY HOUSING COALITION
(Coachella, California)
Farmworker Cooperative Housing Project

The Coachella Valley Housing Coalition (CVHC) has been working with low-income Hispanic farmworkers living in substandard mobile home parks to help them form a cooperative and to develop a new mobile home park to be owned by the cooperative. The families have formed a cooperative (La Cooperative La Esperanza), have elected a board of directors, and hold regular meetings. Thus far, CVHC has helped the cooperative receive a $300,000 state Farmworker Housing Grant to be used for land acquisition and construction costs. Total project development costs will be approximately $650,000. CVHC will continue to assist the cooperative in securing the additional funding, in closing escrow on the land site, and in constructing the housing project. [CHD]

Hispanic communications networks

Radio stations and publications owned and run by Hispanics have played important roles on the West Coast in establishing communications among far-flung agricultural workers. Centro Campesino is a natural outgrowth of the ability to reach out to members of the Hispanic community, and the Saguache project is a good example of the many needs to be served.

NORTHWEST CHICANO RADIO NETWORK
(Granger, Washington)

Centro Campesino is a two-year-old farmworker membership association. Its goal is to develop the leadership and organizing skills of the Yakima Valley farmworkers community and to organize the community into a cohesive sociopolitical unit. It has established a membership base of 1,500 farmworker families (7,000 individuals) and a Farmworker Organizing Council of 12 farmworkers. Centro's organizing efforts will continue to deal with such problems as low wages, loss of unemployment benefits due to inaccurate reporting by growers, inability of farmworkers to obtain unemployment because of state laws, exclusion of farmworkers from basic worker rights legislation, and assistance with the new immigration bill. [CHD]

SAGUACHE COUNTY COMMUNITY COUNCIL
(Center, Colorado)
Center Community Education/Action Project

The Saguache County Community Council (SCCC) is an organization of 200 low-income Chicanos who have addressed the problems of poor people in Center, Colorado, for the past nineteen years. With the Center Community Education/Action Project, it has focused its efforts on creating equality of educational opportunity in the Center School System. In support of this, it publishes *Carnales Unidos*, a community paper. Additionally, SCCC has sponsored a solar energy economic development project and Artes del Valle, a craft cooperative. It has provided jobs for local people through programs such as Public Service Employment, on-the-job training, CETA dropout, and work experience programs. Also, SCCC forced the School Board to redistrict in 1981, creating a Chicano seat. [CHD]

Grants to Asian Groups

Grants to Asian organizations are usually directed to a particular group, Cambodian or Hmong refugees, Hawaiians, Filipinos, and so on. Only a few such grants were made by CHD; many more were made by the Women's Foundation in California. The following grant is typical of the problems these grants help tackle.

ASIAN IMMIGRANT WOMEN ADVOCATES
(Oakland, California)
Organizing Project of Unskilled Asian Immigrant
Women Workers

This project will focus on the problems of unskilled Asian immigrant women workers in the San Francisco Bay area, especially problems of education and employment. The primary goal is to educate the members on their rights as workers, immigrants, and women and to provide the leadership development needed to conduct self-advocacy and collective bargaining to improve wages and working conditions. Asian Immigrant Women Advocates has conducted successful grass-roots organizing efforts among Chinese, Korean, Vietnamese and Filipino hotel, garment, restaurant, and nursing home workers so that they can have a voice in the decisions that govern their lives. It has developed a base of 350 worker-members, which is evolving into an ongoing coalition made up of both unionized and nonunionized workers. [CHD]

Grants to Improve the Economy of the South

Throughout the twentieth century, the South has been an economic battleground and the object, generation after generation, of campaigns for a "new South." The current campaigns find many Southern communities newly impoverished by plant closures, impacted by industrial pollutants, and in great need of more effective governmental and industrial policies. Grants to help in these situations have long been high on the agendas of progressive social change funders, who are sensitive of the extent to which psychological and spiritual factors may determine the outcome of the struggle to survive and prosper in a difficult economic and ecologically threatened environment.

COMMISSION ON RELIGION IN APPALACHIA
(Nashville, Tennessee)
Economic Transformation Committee

The Commission on Religion in Appalachia is a coalition of eighteen major denominations and ten state councils, which has been addressing the social and economic problems of Appalachia for over twenty-two years. The commission's Economic Transformation Committee is analyzing the causes and effects of the region's economic crisis and devising strategies for practical solutions. [TYP]

SOUTHERN EMPOWERMENT PROJECT
(Inez, Kentucky)

The Southern Empowerment Project is a consortium of organizations, formed in 1985, that seeks to overcome institutional and systemic abuses in the South that prevent low-income community organizations from achieving broad empowerment of low-income people. The project confronts the systemic causes of racism, poverty, and isolation in the upper South. It seeks to build deeper institutional support for community organizing goals by encouraging the development of capable organizers connected to one another through an understanding of Southern institutions and systems, and by integrating the diverse points of view of existing organizations into a coherent analysis and strategy for institutional and systemic change. [CHD]

TENNESSEE TAX PROJECT
(Nashville, Tennessee)
Tax Reform Research Project

The Tennessee Tax Project seeks to increase public support for progressive tax reform in Tennessee by researching current tax policies, analyzing the impact of potential changes, and conducting media and educational activities around tax issues. [TYP]

Grants Concerning the Farm Crisis in America

My files contain over fifty grants to organizations in a score of states heavily dependent on agriculture (and some to policy centers in the nation's capital), illustrating how the progressive social change community reacts to crisis. The plight of family farms, the impact of banking practices on the availability of credit, and the extensive use of pesticides by agribusiness are seen as issues to be used as organizing tools and as spurs to the search for long-term answers on the part of both farming communities and government.

PRAIRIEFIRE RURAL ACTION, INC.
(Des Moines, Iowa)
The American Farm Crisis Project

Since mid–1983, the American Farm Crisis Project has been organizing farm and rural people in Iowa—one of the states hardest hit by the farm crisis. The project has facilitated the growth of the project to ten statewide farm, labor, church, and community organizations and the expansion of local, grass-roots Farm Unity Survival Committees to some forty-five Iowa counties. The project has become nationally recognized for its role as a credible and increasingly powerful voice for family farm agriculture and rural communities, and has focused its organizing and institutional change efforts at the local, state, and national levels. The project is operated under the auspices of Prairiefire Rural Action Inc., a nonprofit rural education, organizing, advocacy, and training organization based in Des Moines. [CHD]

SMALL FARM VIABILITY PROJECT (SFVP)
(Stockton, California)

The Small Farm Viability Project (SFVP) is a collaborative effort of the Diocese of Stockton, the Stockton Farmers Cooperative, and the American Friends Service Committee. During the first year, the project will concentrate on increasing the viability of the Stockton Farmers Cooperative. The cooperative has a multiethnic membership of limited resource farmers. The San Joaquin County area is increasingly dominated by larger agribusiness concerns that have, in effect, forced many family farms to go under. Through innovative marketing and through the production of specialty crops, the small farmers will now have the opportunity to survive. The SFVP is also developing the Demonstration Farm, which will test the production of new ethnic vegetables and research organic farming techniques that will give the members of the cooperative an advantage in the marketplace. A third component, the Entry Level Farm, will train minorities and women who want to become productive farmers. [CHD]

ILLINOIS FARM ALLIANCE
(Edwardsville, Illinois)
Rural Organizing Project

The Illinois Farm Alliance is a coalition of progressive farm organizations and citizen groups. The alliance has a long list of accomplishments: the development and enactment of a landmark farmland assessment law, the initiation of a "hot line" for financially pressed farmers, successful actions preventing lenders from foreclosure, and the establishment of a state insurance fund to protect farmers from grain elevator bankruptcy. It also has aided the members of a rural electric cooperative to defeat unresponsive directors and elect a majority of sympathetic candidates to their co-op's board. The alliance is a recognized and successful advocate of policies to help economically pressed farmers and rural citizens. The goal of the Rural Organizing Project is to help farmers and rural people build effective citizen organizations, so they can have a strong voice in the institutions that dominate their lives. [CHD]

MINNESOTA GROUNDSWELL
(Lamberton, Minnesota)
Save Rural Minnesota

Minnesota Groundswell is a grass-roots coalition of farmers and rural citizens, from various organizations, who are committed to building a movement that can achieve solutions to the crisis in rural America. A membership organization, begun in 1984, Groundswell now has active chapters in over forty rural counties. Organizing has focused on the following: (1) advocacy and direct relief—chapters provide "hot-line" support to farm families in personal and financial distress; (2) public rallies and protest—it organizes public protest when it is a means to correct an abuse; (3) community education/coalition building—chapters organize public meetings and actions that educate and train rural communities on rural policy issues; and (4) legislative/institutional change—it assists local leadership in organizing efforts to change public and institutional policies. [CHD]

Grants Concerning National Economic Revitalization

Reindustrialization and labor studies

As the national debates proceed in both ecclesiastic and secular circles about the role of a worker in society (as well as about the relation of the American economy to the world economy, the competition with the Japanese, and the need for restructuring and revitalization of manufacturing and service industries), many different kinds of grant applications come to the funders' attention. Some use the vocabulary of economic justice, plant closings, conversion from defense to civilian employment, new forms of labor-management relations, and new criteria of economic development. Some seek assistance for small, usually cooperative, enterprises. The selection of grants that follows illustrates the range of possibilities.

THE MICAH PROJECT
(Allentown, Pennsylvania)
Lehigh Valley Project

The goal of the MICAH Project is to build a coalition and power base from which to address local plant closings and to devise viable, just alternatives such as worker buy-outs and local ownership. The model is the Naugatuck Valley Project. MICAH seeks to develop strong local leadership among displaced workers and those threatened with displacement, to build bridges between labor and business, and to build a strong base from which local churches can address the area's economic distress. Project participants are local churches, individuals, labor officials, and activists. [CHD]

PLANT CLOSURES PROJECT
(Oakland, California)
Economic Justice Coalition of Oakland

The Economic Justice Coalition of Oakland (EJCO) will unite diverse Bay Area people and groups in specific campaigns to save both service sector and industrial jobs in Oakland. The Plant Closures Project—a labor, religious, community alliance—helps communities and workers fight closures, educates the public about causes/effects of job loss, and works to develop/implement just economic policies to address needs of poor people and communities. Since 1981, the project has helped organize anticlosure campaigns at ten area companies. [CHD]

MIDWEST CENTER FOR LABOR RESEARCH
(Chicago, Illinois)
Plant Closure Research

The Midwest Center for Labor Research is an effort by community, labor, and business leaders in Chicago to research the consequences of plant closings and to develop job saving and job creating strategies for industrial communities throughout the region. [TYP]

SAN ANTONIO COMMUNITIES ORGANIZED FOR
PUBLIC SERVICE
(San Antonio, Texas)
Worker Association Strategy

The twelve-year-old Communities Organized for Public Service (COPS) is a broad-based organization composed of more than 90,000 families. COPS is at the forefront of such issues as urban sprawl, re-

districting, utility rate increases, voter registration, economic development, education reform, and employment. In this project, COPS is
addressing the issues of unemployment and underemployment. It has
succeeded in bringing together workers in the garment district. The
Worker Association Strategy calls for developing leadership among
workers. The project will work on the following: (1) identifying, inter-
viewing, and developing leadership among workers in the target area;
(2) forming worker associations that will be integrated into the organization; (3) addressing community issues and issues dealing with the
workplace; (4) continuing to mount voter registration and voter turnout
campaigns; (5) establishing a corporate responsibility strategy to initiate
changes in the workplace consistent with church teachings. [CHD]

NAUGATUCK VALLEY PROJECT
(Waterbury, Connecticut)

The Naugatuck Valley Project is a coalition of local unions, churches,
and community organizations joined together to deal with plant closing
and long-term disinvestment in the Naugatuck Valley, one of the oldest
industrial areas in the nation. It has drawn together a wide array of
local grass-roots leaders in fifty member-group organizations to gain a
voice in dealing with multinational corporations in fourteen threatened
or actual closings. Its greatest accomplishment has been to organize the
community and play a pivotal role as catalyst in the sale of the Bridgeport Brass Company to its employees. This saved 225 jobs and has led
to work with five other potential buy-outs, at companies employing
over 1,000 workers. Goals in the coming year are to organize in poorer
sections of the valley; to create jobs through employee-owned, start-
up companies; and to develop a local source of financing to assist lower
income employees in meeting their equity needs in employee buy-outs.
[CHD]

TRI-STATE CONFERENCE ON STEEL
(Pittsburgh, Pennsylvania)
Steel Valley Authority

The Tri-State Conference on Steel is a community-based, public interest organization that promotes alternative economic plans of reinvestment in abandoned industrial facilities in western Pennsylvania. It

organized the formation of a "Steel Valley Authority," with the power of eminent domain to acquire, hold, or broker abandoned industrial facilities to third parties or employee buy-outs. The Steel Valley Authority (SVA) project seeks to secure community input into the decision-making process of the authority's appointed board. The project also seeks to lay the groundwork for future plant closing/reopening efforts in the Man Valley. Project goals are (1) to build six active SVA Residents Committees, (2) to solicit the participation of three additional communities as official SVA members, (3) to lay the groundwork for four plant closing struggles, and (4) to support the SVA in its first project to maintain or reopen an industrial facility. [CHD]

Women's economic status

Many grants in my files are focused on women's economic issues, all in the context of the national economic debates I have described previously. Some of the grants were made to projects at the NAACP, concerning black women's rights, and at the National Women's Law Center. Some are grants to assist women-owned enterprises.

WOMEN'S ECONOMIC AGENDA PROJECT
(Oakland, California)
Outreach and Education Project

The Women's Economic Agenda Project (WEAP) is a broad-based organization of California women working together to reverse the current and steady decline in the economic status of women and children. Participants in the project are actively organizing throughout the state to define clearly their economic needs, to propose constructive social and institutional changes to remedy these needs, and to develop community and state action plans to implement such changes. The project, which unites women on fundamental common economic concerns, is comprised of a heterogeneous mix of women from diverse backgrounds. WEAP's goals are to continue extensive outreach and education on the increasing impoverishment of women and children, recommending model policy and community action to reverse the trend of the feminization of poverty. [CHD]

WESTSIDE PARISH COALITION
(San Antonio, Texas)
Construction Worker Cooperative

The Westside Parish Coalition is a group of six Catholic Churches on San Antonio's Hispanic westside working to improve the quality of life for over 28,000 residents. Ongoing projects have centered on the feminization of poverty and its elimination through employment training, basic education, and job placement. The Construction Workers Cooperative will form a construction company under the control of its workers—primarily single women—who are now completing the Coalition's Ventures in Community Improvements program. The cooperative will allow the women to improve their skills and performance and to obtain working knowledge of the competitive market, while serving as subcontractors to the coalition in its residential construction project. Jobs will be developed through new construction, trainees will move from subsidized to unsubsidized employment, and the co-op will move into increasingly competitive situations. [CHD]

Other Grants for Housing and Community Development

Housing and development issues are present in many of the grants already described, especially in minorities' communities. Salvaging public housing for low-income families is a current need. So too is the demand for socially responsible investments, as exemplified by the activities of the Archdiocese of New York examined next. Grants in my file also went to studies for better housing and housing finance policies being conducted by the Institute for Policy Studies and the Southern Finance Project.

THE HOUSING FUND OF THE ARCHDIOCESE OF NEW YORK
(New York, New York)
Diocesan Development Project

The Housing Fund of the Archdiocese of New York was begun to promote and develop low-income housing in the five targeted communities. The development project includes three components: the Homeownership Project, the Homesteader Program, and the Housing

Fund. The Housing Fund was begun with a $1 million investment from the Archdiocese of New York. The fund provides below-market rate mortgages to the housing projects. By providing this piece of financing, other government and private monies can be leveraged to maintain affordable prices for the houses. Renovation on almost 300 units is progressing. The first loans have been disbursed for approximately 40 units in three different communities. Approximately $6 million in state and city funds has been leveraged through the project. [CHD]

NATIONAL TRAINING AND INFORMATION CENTER

(Chicago, Illinois)

Financial Industry Partnership Project

A major goal of the National Training and Information Center (NTIC) through its Financial Industry Partnership Project is to create local partnerships between community organizations and private institutions (such as banks) that determine the economic stability of neighborhoods. NTIC has trained local organizations in four cities in the use of the Community Reinvestment Act. As a result of its assistance, four reinvestment agreements have been reached; $110 million in affordable credit for housing and business development has been made available in low- and moderate-income areas. Agreements have been reached in three additional cities with implementation to follow. In the year ahead, NTIC will expand its training to three new national sites. Goals of this expansion are to create three new reinvestment partnerships and to train nonwhite leaders in disenfranchised communities in development methods and resources. [CHD]

SOUTH CAROLINA FAIR SHARE

(Charleston, South Carolina)

Public Housing Organizing Project

South Carolina Fair Share is a multi-issue, citizen coalition recently launched to develop and act on a statewide progressive agenda for South Carolina. Its first organizing project will bring low- and moderate-income persons from throughout Charleston County together to work for the preservation and improvement of public housing. [TYP]

Grants Concerning Environmental Quality

The opportunities to organize around practical and ethical issues concerning the environment escalated during the 1980s as people became aware of the consequences of toxic chemicals, nuclear waste, management practices affecting the nation's public lands, and acid rain, to name a few. Many of the grants were to local organizations. Representative grants to regional and national groups follow.

NORTH AMERICAN CONFERENCE ON CHRISTIANITY AND ECOLOGY

(San Francisco, California)

Appalachia-Science in the Public Interest

The purpose of the conference was to elucidate the ecological dimensions inherent in the Christian faith. Bringing an ecological dimension to the Christian church represents an innovative and powerful tool to marshal concern for earth healing. [THR]

CITIZENS CLEARINGHOUSE FOR HAZARDOUS WASTE, INC.

(Arlington, Virginia)

Outreach to Low-Income & Minority Communities

Formed in 1981 by veterans of the Love Canal fight, Citizens Clearinghouse for Hazardous Wastes, Inc. (CCHW) helps local grass-roots leaders organize their communities to fight the unsafe disposal of toxic wastes. Its membership consists of over 1,000 community organizations from across the country. It helps these grass-roots groups by providing them with the tools necessary to win victories at the local level. CCHW's overall goal is to end the irresponsible management of toxic materials nationwide. Two field organizers for CCHW work closely with new and existing grass-roots groups in areas of the country that are particularly attractive to toxic dumpers. [CHD]

LOUISIANA ENVIRONMENTAL ACTION
NETWORK
(Baton Rouge, Louisiana)

The Louisiana Environmental Action Network (LEAN), an organization of both grass-roots groups and individuals, has been responsible for stopping the siting of numerous wastehandling facilities and was instrumental in saving the state's environmental agency from budget cuts. LEAN serves as a clearinghouse and organizing focus for fifty-plus grass-roots groups statewide. It seeks changes in the state's relevant laws and regulations, and it seeks to educate and involve citizens in those changes. LEAN's Louisiana Environmental Organizing Project will educate and organize the rural poor in order to keep Louisiana from becoming the waste dumping ground of America. It aims to move toward cleaning up the state's land, air, and water. Through a series of technical workshops and skills-training sessions, LEAN will provide the tools necessary for organized action. Coordinated vigils and rallies will support the process. [CHD]

TEXAS CENTER FOR RURAL STUDIES
(Austin, Texas)
Environment/Health Protection Organizing Project

The Texas Center for Rural Studies is a statewide research action organization mobilizing citizens around a range of natural resource and related health and environmental problems, specifically the health hazards of toxic waste and pesticides. [TYP and JFS]

RADIATION RESEARCH PROJECT
(Knoxville, Tennessee)

The Radiation Research Project documents the federal government's suppression of medical and legal information concerning the effects of radiation exposure on communities, atomic veterans, and nuclear production workers. [TYP]

Some Grants Concerning Health, Education, and Welfare

The grants made by the funders in my sample are not as compelling as might be expected, and none of the projects seemed noteworthy enough to include in this chapter. CHD itself identified only a few grants in the health field, which, of course, is a prime target of funders willing to finance service providers. The grants in my sample, however, range widely, concerned with the rights of seniors, disabled persons, victims of AIDS, workers in health agencies, and families of prisoners. Public education systems, although they do not appear to be serving the needs of low-income and minority populations generally, are only now beginning to be the subject of community-organizing campaigns, but a number of grants provide assistance to adult literacy and related programs. Women's health issues are covered in the next section.

Other Grants Concerning Rights, Especially Women's

A multitude of topical grants have been made to such organizations as the American Civil Liberties Union and the Center for Constitutional Rights for educational projects related to the nomination of Robert Bork to the Supreme Court and to other threats to civil liberties, including the rights of prisoners facing the death penalty and of the homeless. A number of grants concerned the rights of women, especially blacks, to adequate health care. An abiding topic in the women's health care field has to do with reproductive rights, a topic that does not fall within CHD's guidelines but that attracts a number of the other funders I surveyed. Examples of such grants follow.

NATIONAL UNION OF THE HOMELESS INC.
(Philadelphia, Pennsylvania)

The National Union of the Homeless Inc. was founded in 1985 to organize and mobilize homeless men and women to speak for themselves and lead the push for improvements and changes in policies and programs that affect their quality of life. With affiliates in eight cities, it is the only membership-based, advocacy organization in the nation that is founded, managed, and operated by homeless people. Successes include: (1) the "legal" right and mandate that city government provide shelter; (2) a court decision upholding the right to register to vote, absent a permanent residential address; (3) changes in food stamp and income assistance policies that previously discriminated against the homeless;

and (4) affirmative action employment of the homeless in city contracted agencies that serve homeless clients. In 1987 the union will organize affiliates in eight additional cities and expand technical support for homeless activists. [CHD]

9 TO 5, NATIONAL ASSOCIATION FOR WORKING WOMEN
(Cleveland, Ohio)
Organizing Low-Income Women Working 9 to 5

The National Association of Working Women will continue to expand activities to new targeted cities and states to (a) build self-sufficient grass-roots organizations that will help working women improve their working conditions, (b) promote policy changes in the workplace and on the local and state levels that will benefit them, and (c) influence public policy and public opinion on working women's issues. The group's project will develop model programs to deal with critical issues that affect low-income working women, including: (a) pay equity; (b) new clerical employment trends that threaten job loss, less access to promotions and training, and declining wages in a work sector that already is at poverty levels; and (c) worsening discrimination towards minority and older women. [CHD]

MS. FOUNDATION FOR WOMEN
(New York, New York)
Women of Color Projects/General Support

- For direct grants to projects run by and primarily benefiting women of color ($30,000) and for general support of the Foundation's technical assistance work with these projects. [JFS]
- For the Resource Committee on Reproductive Health Care's efforts to increase the funding community's awareness and support of work to ensure reproductive freedom. [JFS]
- For distribution of their resource book, *Women of Color—Building Bridges between Resources and Needs*, an effort to increase support for women of color projects and to educate funders on the issues and concerns of these women. [JFS]
- For the Foundation's endowment campaign. The income from this grant is to be used for projects benefitting women of color. [JFS]

RELIGIOUS COALITION FOR ABORTION RIGHTS
(Washington, D.C.)
Educational Fund

The group aims to support the Women of Color Partnership Project's efforts to increase the participation of women of color in prochoice issues and in the prochoice movement. [JFS]

Topical Grants for Voter Registration Drives

Voting rights campaigns have been funded since the beginning of the progressive social change movement in the 1960s but claimed a prominent place on the funders' agendas as the percentage of eligible voters actually voting continued to decline and after President Reagan took office. In addition to the grants that follow, grants for registration campaigns in the Carolinas, the Midwest, Mississippi, and Alabama and grants for the work of the League of Rural Voters, the NAACP's Legal Defense Fund, the Southern Rural Voters, and the Campaign for a New South were represented in my file. Individuals funded a number of related organizations that did not quality for tax-exempt status. Whether these funders will continue to fund such campaigns depends now upon their evaluations of the 1988 races, which produced a number of local victories although considerable disappointment with the results at the national level.

PROJECT VOTE!
(Washington, D.C.)

Project VOTE! was created in June 1982 to help build the power of the poor through a comprehensive program of voter registration and issue-oriented voter education. Its goals are to empower poor people by (1) registering them to vote, (2) increasing the number of poor people actually voting, and (3) to do the above in such a way as to strengthen local community organizations and coalitions making it possible for them to effectively hold governmental officials accountable to the needs of their community. In addition, Project VOTE! has provided technical assistance, staffing, and a model that has played a key role in registering and turning out hundreds of thousands of additional voters. [CHD]

CENTER FOR CONSTITUTIONAL RIGHTS
(Greenville, Mississippi)
Mississippi Voting Rights Project

The Mississippi Voting Rights Project (MVRP) is a statewide effort to break down barriers to equal rights and equal power for self-determination in the state of Mississippi. MVRP is now working in eighteen of the state's poorest counties and is working statewide on complex issues of discrimination against black voters. The project has won victories in a wide variety of cases including: annexation; at-large, county election commissions; school board challenges; redistricting; majority vote; and misdirection of public school funds. In 1986 racial gerrymandering in thirteen counties was replaced with new nondiscriminatory plans that do not dilute black voting strength. Project goals include more access to jobs and financial resources, successful representative elections, making community officials responsive to community needs, and stopping diversion of public resources into private segregated institutions. [CHD]

NORTHWEST COMMUNITIES PROJECT
(Portland, Oregon)

The Northwest Voter Registration/Education Project is a project of the Northwest Communities Project. It is a regional voter registration/education organization working in six states of the northwest United States. Its goal is the empowerment of low-income and multiethnic peoples by means of increasing the level of citizen participation. The long-range goal will be achieved through intensive voter registration/education campaigns, leadership training, citizenship and system literacy training, and voter education on vital issues. In addition, the project will develop a data base on voter registration statistics for ethnic communities and by economic and age factors. It will analyze turnout percentages and will identify any legal barriers to voter registration and citizen participation. [CHD]

L.A. JOBS WITH PEACE
(Los Angeles, California)

L.A. Jobs with Peace is both a membership organization and a coalition based in the predominantly black and Latino communities of south and east Los Angeles. The goal of the Neighborhood Organizing Project is that neighborhood participants will select, research, and plan an action campaign to change a self-identified problem in the community and be trained in how to conduct a series of neighborhood organizing drives to build the organization necessary to win the change. In the last five years, L.A. Jobs with Peace has built a neighborhood precinct network of over 700 people, registered over 80,000 new low-income voters, and founded ongoing neighborhood organizations in South, East, and North Los Angeles. [CHD]

Grants Concerning Peace and National Security

Topical grants on Central American issues

Another example of how the social change funders react to current events are the grants made by their foundations to educational projects concerning U.S. policies in Central and South America. The organization listed here is only one of a score of tax-exempt entities funders helped to create. Grants were also made to well-established researchers in universities and think tanks.

WASHINGTON OFFICE ON LATIN AMERICA
(Washington, D.C.)
Central America Organizing Project

The organization monitors human rights practices and political developments in Central America and the formulation and implementation of United States policies toward the region. [JFS and TDS]

On other peace and national security issues

The progressive social change community has been admonished from time to time to think globally and act locally, and hence grants flow to organizations that operate at the local level to stimulate people to organize themselves as voters and spokespersons on defense and foreign-policy matters. By its charter, CHD made no grants on such topics, but the other funders in my file were generous in their support of a wide variety of issue-based projects, including ones abroad. One example of such support follows.

THE TIDES FOUNDATION
(San Francisco, California)
Communications Consortium/Arms Control Media
Project

The Communications Consortium/Arms Control Media Project focuses attention specifically on media coverage of arms control issues and works with grass-roots groups to enable them to communicate information to the press. [TDS]

Other Media Projects

Progressive social change activism generates all sorts of videotapes, movie projects, school curricula, publications, and cultural and arts programs. Not all of them fall within the guidelines of the foundations in my survey, but a few examples of media grants made in support of progressive causes follow.

APPALSHOP, INC.
(Whitesburg, Kentucky)
WMMT Radio

Appalshop is a media and arts center, formed in 1969, that works for social and economic change in the Appalachian coalfields. Its purpose is to communicate issues and to portray traditional values as a way to bring people together. This project will continue the work of WMMT-FM, Appalshop's noncommercial radio station that reaches a ten-county area in Kentucky and Virginia. The station is programmed by volunteers from the primary coverage area. Most of them have received their radio training at the station. WMMT is the only noncommercial radio station that originates in the area and is the only community-based station that can be heard in the region. The station seeks to meet listener needs for locally produced affairs, cultural, and educational programs and for national programs that offer alternative viewpoints not available on local commercial radio. The station went on the air in November 1985. [CHD]

HIGHLANDER RESEARCH AND EDUCATION
CENTER
(New Market, Tennessee)
Appalachian Cultural Organizing Project

The Center works to use Appalachian cultural traditions and music as a means to organize around issues of social and economic injustice throughout the South and Appalachia. [JFS]

THE TIDES FOUNDATION
(San Francisco, California)
Communications Consortium/Media Center

The Communications Consortium/Media Center was established as a media resource center for the public interest community. The Media Center maintains a data base on reporters and other decisionmakers in print and electronic media; monitors media resources and publications, including public opinion surveys; and works with nonprofit organizations to develop skills to more effectively utilize the press to cover progressive issues. [TDS]

Grants to Help Build the Social Change Movement

Grants to increase the number and effectiveness of progressive social change funds are attractive to a number of foundations and individuals. When this was written, the venerable Youth Project, in addition to changing its own name, was terminating the Progressive Constituency Network, whose work may be continued by some other means in the long series of attempts at networking that has characterized the informal internal relationships among members of the movement.

NATIONAL COMMITTEE FOR RESPONSIVE
PHILANTHROPY
(Washington, D.C.)
Alternative Funds Movement Project

The Alternative Funds Movement Project aims to organize nonprofit groups that work for poor people, minorities, women, and others to raise significant new monies from workplace charity drives. One important new revenue source for grass-roots groups is workplace fundraising—getting contributions from workers through payroll deductions. To take advantage of this way to raise money, nonprofits must form federations to collectively gain access to the workplace. The National Committee for Responsive Philanthropy's primary goal in this project is to organize the federations, which it calls "alternative funds." The group's long-term goal of making major reforms in philanthropy will result in more dollars for groups seeking social justice goals, economic self-sufficiency, and political empowerment. [CHD]

WOMEN AND FOUNDATIONS
(New York, New York)
Corporate Philanthropy

This organization provides technical assistance and support to strengthen existing women's funds and to encourage the growth of new funds. This grant was allocated to the National Network of Women's Funds. [JFS]

THE YOUTH PROJECT
(Washington, D.C.)
Progressive Constituency Network

As a complement to our field representatives' support of local, state, and regional organizations, the Progressive Constituency Network (PCN) encouraged disparate issue and constituency groups to increase the effectiveness of their work by identifying and working collaboratively around their common agendas to increase citizen participation in decision-making processes. This year, PCN provided assistance to individual groups and collaborative efforts in several states, helping to build relationships, and providing information, resources, and funds. It also created opportunities for organizers and representatives of the groups it worked with to meet with each other to share ideas and strategies. Michael Ansara served as PCN's coordinator. As well as helping distribute information, PCN provided important opportunities for local and state organizers involved in coalitions and other collaborative efforts to meet, share information about successful strategies and techniques, and explore ways to develop messages and themes with the potential of weaving together the issue agendas of seemingly disparate issue and constituency groups. Three conferences—in October 1987 and February and June 1988—brought together some of the best local and statewide organizers in the country along with important thinkers and policy analysts. These conferences provided a valuable meeting place and forum for stepping away from the day-to-day pressures of organizing and discussing broader issues and strategies. PCN also convened similar meetings, called Washington Forums, at which national organizations shared information and strategies, particularly around voter participation activities. Fiscal year 1987–1988 was PCN's last year as an active special project. At this time, the work of the Progressive Constituency Network has been fully integrated into the work of the Youth Project's field representatives and program director.[3] [TYP and JFS]

Notes

Chapter 1

1. See, for example, Lyman's address to the National Society of Fundraising Executives, Seattle, February 5, 1988.

2. By coincidence, David Freeman's general bibliography on foundations, designed to "define foundations and their role in the larger field of philanthropy and in the society as a whole," in his *Handbook on Private Foundations* (Cabin John, Md.: Seven Locks Press for the Council on Foundations, 1981) is entitled "What's in a Name?"

3. Independent Sector, "The Charitable Behavior of Americans: Findings from a National Survey Conducted by Yankelovich, Skelly and White, Inc., Commissioned by the Rockefeller Brothers Fund," *Independent Sector*, 1828 L Street, Washington, D.C. 20036, 1986. See also Independent Sector's *Giving and Volunteering in the United States: 1988 Summary* (based on a Gallup Organization survey funded by many foundations for the Daring Goals/Give Five program).

4. One example of current effort in this area is Frances Lappe's Public Values Project at her Institute for Food and Development Policy and her related book, *Rediscovering America's Values* (New York: Ballantine Books, 1989). Another example is a book by Harry Boyte, *Commonwealth of Freedom: The Promise of Citizen Politics* (New York: Free Press, 1989).

5. Bay Area Committee for Responsive Philanthropy, *Small Change from Big Bucks: A Report and Recommendations on Bay Area Foundations and Social Change* (San Francisco: Bay Area Committee, 1979), 6.

6. The Foundation Center (79 Fifth Ave., New York, NY 10003) properly describes itself as the nation's number one source of information on foundation and corporate philanthropy. Michael Seltzer's *Securing Your Organization's Future: A Complete Guide to Fundraising Strategies* (1987) was written for The Foundation Center. See also Kim Klein, *Fundraising for Social Change*, 2d ed. (Inverness, Calif.: Chardon Press, 1988) and Joan Flanagan, *The Grass Roots Fundraising Book*, the first edition of which was written for the Youth Project in 1977. See note 8 to Chapter 2 for information on directories of progressive funding sources.

7. Robert Matthews Johnson, *The First Charity: How Philanthropy Can Contribute to Democracy in America* (Cabin John, Md.: Seven Locks Press, 1988), xviii.

8. See Drummond Pike (president of the Tides Foundation, formerly at the Youth Project, and expert in dealing with both funders and grant applicants), "How Foundations Decide Who Gets Their Money," *Whole Earth Review* (Summer 1988): 74–75.

9. See, for instance, Barry D. Karl and Stanley N. Katz, "Foundations and Ruling Class Elites" in a special issue on "Philanthropy, Patronage, Politics," *Daedalus* 116, no. 1 (Winter 1987): 1–40.

10. Joseph Schumpeter, *Capitalism, Socialism and Democracy*, 3d ed. (New York: Harper, 1950).

11. Robert Heilbroner, "The Triumph of Capitalism," *New Yorker Magazine*, January 23, 1989, 98–109.

12. Typical of recent press coverage of studies confirming the widening gap are Martin Tolchin's report on a congressional study (*New York Times*, March 23, 1989, 1), and articles in *Business Week* (April 17, 1989, 17) and by Leonard Silk (*New York Times*, May 12, 1989, C2) commenting on the work of Sheldon Danziger and his colleagues. Evidence that federal transfer payments ameliorate the gap is found in U.S. Department of Commerce, Bureau of the Census, *Measuring the Effect of Benefits and Taxes on Income and Poverty—1986*, Consumer Income Series P–60, no. 164–RD–1 (Washington, D.C.: 1988).

13. John B. Judis, "Capitalism redux, or does it really," *In These Times*, June 21–July 4, 1989, 2.

Chapter 2

1. Johnson, *First Charity*, 101.

2. Bay Area Committee, *Small Change*, 12.

3. See Virginia A. Hodgkinson, "Academic Centers and Research Institutes Focusing on the Study of Philanthropy, Voluntarism, and Not-for-Profit Activity: A Progress Report," *Independent Sector* (November 1988).

4. The most extensive use of data in the Master File is Virginia A. Hodgkinson and Murray S. Weitzman, *Dimensions of the Independent Sector: A Statistical Profile*, 2d ed. (Washington, D.C.: Independent Sector, 1986), 17–18, tables 1.4, 1.6.

5. See Margaret Riley, "A Private Foundation Profile for 1983," *SOI Bulletin* 6, no. 3 (Winter 1986–1987): 11–24 and Cecilia Hilgert, "Nonprofit Charitable Organizations, 1983," *SOI Bulletin* 6, no. 4 (Spring 1987): 31–42. For more detailed references to IRS regulations, see Chapter 11, note 2 (Odendahl) and note 5 (Citizen Vote, Inc.).

6. Hilgert, "Nonprofit Charitable Organizations," 31.

7. National Center for Charitable Statistics, *National Taxonomy of Exempt Entities (NTEE): A System for Classifying Nongovernmental, Nonbusiness Tax-Exempt Organizations in the U.S. with a focus on IRS Section 501(c)(3) Philanthropic Organizations*, developed by the National Center for Charitable Statistics, a program of Independent Sector, Washington, D.C. (1987).

8. A selected list of directories of progressive social change funders:

—Jill R. Shellow, ed., *Grant Seekers Guide: Funding Sourcebook* (Mt. Kisco, N.Y.: Moyer Bell for the National Network of Grantmakers, 1985).

—Public Media Center, *Index of Progressive Funders* (San Francisco, Calif.: Public Media Center, 1985).

—Gary Delgado, *Activist's Guide to Religious Funders: Leveraging God's Resources from Her Representatives on Earth: A Working Model* (Oakland, Calif.: Center for Third World Organizing, 1987).

—Taft Group, *Fund Raiser's Guide to Religious Philanthropy* (Washington, D.C.: Taft Group, 1987).

—Taft Group, *Fund Raiser's Guide to Private Fortunes* (Washington, D.C.: Taft Group, 1987).

9. For more information, write The Funding Exchange, 666 Broadway, #500, New York, NY 10012.

10. The Data Center's address is 464 19th Street, Oakland, CA 94612, the Interfaith Center's is 475 Riverside Drive, New York, NY 10115. Regarding the capital markets, see, for example, Co-Op America, "A Socially Responsible Financing Planning Guide," *Building Economic Alternatives* (Fall 1988) published by Co-Op America (2100 M St., Washington, D.C., 20063. Also see Severyn T. Bruyn, *The Field of Social Investment* (New York: Cambridge University Press, 1987).

11. Robert Zevin in *Directory of Socially Responsible Investments* (New York: Funding Exchange and Bread & Roses Community Fund, 1983), 3–5, reprinted in second edition, 1986, prepared by the Institute for Community Economics and the Funding Exchange. See also John G. Simon (the president of the Taconic Foundation), "Program-related Investments," Appendix 6 in David E. Freeman, *The Handbook of Private Foundations* (Cabin John, Md.: Seven Oaks Press, 1981).

12. Institute for Community Economics, 151 Montague City Road, Greenfield, MA 01301.

13. For more information, write Social Venture Network, 140 East 58th Street, New York, NY 10022.

Chapter 3

1. Independent Sector, *From Belief to Commitment: The Activities and Expenditures of Religious Congregations in the United States*, Summary Report of the Independent Sector (Washington, D.C.: December 1988).

2. Based on revenues in Table 1 (1983) in Riley, "Private Foundation Profile," and Table 2.11 (1982) in Hodgkinson and Weitzman, *Dimensions*, 43, compared to data from *National Data Book* in my Table 3.2.

3. Data from Riley, "Private Foundation Profile," 11 and Table 1.

4. Teresa Odendahl, ed., *America's Wealthy and the Future of Foundations* (New York: Foundation Center, 1987), 2. The study at Yale was funded by W. K. Kellogg Foundation, Andrew W. Mellon Foundation, Charles Stewart Mott Foundation, and the Ford Foundation. The book includes an excellent bibliography on foundations and charitable giving by the wealthy.

5. Odendahl, *America's Wealthy*, 21.

6. J. Craig Jenkins, "Foundation Funding of Progressive Social Movements," in *Grant Seekers Funding Sourcebook*, ed. Jill R. Shellow (Mt. Kisco, N.Y.: Moyer Bell, 1985), *Guide*: 9.

Chapter 4

1. An important book on this general subject is Richard Hofstadter, *Social Darwinism in American Thought* (Boston: Beacon Press, 1955).

2. From Albert M. Sacks, "The Role of Philanthropy: An Institutional View," *Virginia Law Review* 46 (1960): 516, 529 quoted in John G. Simon, "Foundations and Public Controversy: An Affirmative View," in *The Future of Foundations*, ed. Fritz Heimann (Englewood Cliffs, N.J.: Prentice-Hall for the American Assembly, Columbia University, 1973), 60.

3. In F. Emerson Andrews, *Foundation Watcher* (Lancaster, Pa.: Princeton University Press, 1973): 67.

4. Ibid., 37.

5. Ibid., 140ff, 170ff.

6. Jeffrey Hart, "Foundations and Social Activism: A Critical View," in *The Future of Foundations*, ed. Fritz Heimann (Englewood Cliffs, N.J.: Prentice-Hall, 1973).

7. Heimann, *Future*, 123, 172.

8. Waldemar Nielsen, *The Golden Donors* (New York: Truman Talley Books, 1985), 30, 33.

9. Ibid., 7, 137.

10. Ibid., 40–58.

11. Simon, "Foundations and Controversy," 99. Nielsen, *Golden Donors*, 433.

12. Kathleen Teltsch, "Rockefeller Foundation Turns to the Underclass," *New York Times*, January 22, 1989, 24.

13. Nielsen, *Golden Donors*, 138, 144.

14. See discussion of the Garland Foundation in Richard Klugar, *Simple Justice* (New York: Random House, 1977), 132–8.

15. John Friedmann and Clyde Weaver, *Territory and Function* (Berkeley, Calif.: University of California Press, 1979).

16. Frank Adams with Myles Horton, *Unearthing Seeds of Fire: The Idea of Highlander* (Winston-Salem, N.C.: John F. Blair, 1975), 110 and John M. Glen, *Highlander: No Ordinary School, 1932–1962* (Lexington, Ky.: University Press of Kentucky, 1988), 171.

17. Michael Harrington, *The Other America: Poverty in the United States* (New York: Macmillan, 1962).

18. Youth Project, *Community Organizing: A Retrospective on Support by the Youth Project, 1970–1984* (Washington, D.C.: Youth Project, 1984), 4. The Youth Project's current address is 2335 18th Street NW, Washington, D.C. 20009. Although the Youth Project's board voted in mid–1989 to change the name of the organization to Partnership for Democracy, I have retained the older, more familiar, name throughout this book.

19. J. Craig Jenkins, "Foundation Funding of Progressive Social Movements," in *Grant Seekers Guide: Funding Sourcebook*, ed. Jill R. Shellow (Mt. Kisco, N.Y.: Moyer Bell, 1985).

20. Odendahl, *America's Wealthy*, ch. 9.

21. DJB Foundation, "Statement of the Board," in *Report of the DJB Foundation, 1971–1975* (Scarsdale, N.Y.: DJB Foundation, 1975), 5ff. The board members were Carol Bernstein Ferry, Robert S. Browne, W. H. Ferry, and Stephen R. Abrams.

22. Marcus Raskin and Chester Hartman, eds., *Winning America: Ideas and Leadership for the 1990's* (Boston, Mass.: South End Press and the Institute for Policy Studies, 1988). The address of the Institute for Policy Studies is 1601 Connecticut Avenue NW, Washington, DC 20009.

Chapter 5

1. From an announcement for "Philanthropy and the Religious Tradition," a forum presented by Independent Sector and United Way Institute, March 1989, Chicago, Ill.

2. For more information on corporate philanthropy, see Hodgkinson and Weitzman, *Dimensions* 49 and publications of the Foundation Center.

3. See, for example, Russell D. Roberts, "Why Do We Feel Guilty Tipping Less Than 15%" *Wall Street Journal*, November 25, 1986, 28.

4. See also Bok's article, "A Daring and Complicated Strategy: Harvard's Effort to Build a First-rate School for Government Service," *Harvard Magazine* (May–June 1989): 49–58.

5. These excerpts and the ones following are from Dr. William Sloane Coffin, Jr., "Justice, Not Charity" (Speech to *Outward Bound International Conference*, September 10, 1988).

6. United States Catholic Conference, *Daring to Seek Justice: People Working Together: The Story of the Campaign for Human Development: Its Roots, Its Programs and Its Challenges* (Washington, D.C.: United States Catholic Conference, 1986), iv.

7. Ibid., vi.

8. Ibid., 17.

9. In reviewing Nelson W. Aldrich, Jr.'s, *Old Money: The Mythology of America's Upper Class* (New York: Knopf, 1988) for *Harvard Magazine* (May–June 1989), Richard Marius recalls Castiglione's fifteenth century *Book of the Courtier* and predicts that *Old Money* will be a comparable best-seller for the Yuppie " 'Market Man,' the new rich, the ambitious and eager entrepreneur clawing his way up," to where Aldrich says the heirs of old money live by myths and codes that help them to believe themselves worthy of their place in the world. And see Adam Hochschild, *Half the Way Home: A Memoir of Father and Son* (New York: Penguin Books, 1987).

10. Odendahl, *America's Wealthy*, xv.

11. Ibid., 5 (and see Chapter 7).

12. Ibid., 228ff.

13. Ibid., 228.

14. DJB Foundation, Report, 6.

15. Paul G. Schervish and Andrew Herman, *The Study on Wealth and Philanthropy: Final Report* (Chestnut Hill, Mass.: Social Welfare Research Institute, Boston College, 1988).

16. Ibid., 43.

17. Ibid., 46.

18. Ibid., 56.

19. Ibid., 168ff.

20. Ibid., 60.

21. Vanguard Public Foundation, *Robin Hood Was Right: A Guide to Giving Your Money for Social Change* (San Francisco, Calif.: Vanguard Public Foundation, 1977).

22. Shellow, *Grantseekers Guide*, 208.

Chapter 6

1. DJB Foundation, *Report*, 7.

2. USCC, *Daring*, 57, 61.

3. Ibid., 53, 62ff.

4. Ibid., 54.

Chapter 7

1. See Chapter 2, note 7.

2. See Chapter 4, note 22.

Chapter 8

1. Johnson, *First Charity*, 38. And see his Chapter 8.

2. Drummond Pike, "How Foundations Decide," 74–75.

3. Drummond Pike, in his introduction to materials for financial statement analysis to be performed by foundations evaluating grant proposals. The materials were prepared by Michael Edwards for private circulation by the Tides Foundation. For further information, write the Foundation at 1388 Sutter Street, San Francisco, CA 94109.

4. My search of college and graduate school directories, however, revealed only one institution currently offering a degree program.

Chapter 9

1. Hyman Bookbinder, "Did the War on Poverty Fail?" *New York Times*, August 20, 1989, E23.

2. Charles Merrill, *The Checkbook: The Politics and Ethics of Foundation Philanthropy* (Boston, Mass.: Oelgeschlager, Gunn & Hain, 1986), 18–20.

3. *National Conference of Catholic Bishops*, A Report on the Campaign for Human Development: An Assessment and Strategic Plan (Paper presented to the NCCB/USCC General Conference, Washington, D.C., November 1988) 224–330 in agenda documentation.

4. Ibid., 227.

5. The several quotations in the pages that follow are taken from David Hunter's speech as published in the Winter 1987 issue of *The Network*, the newsletter of The National Network of Grantmakers, 2000 P Street, NW, Washington, D.C. 20036.

Chapter 10

1. Citizens Information Service of Illinois, 332 S. Michigan Ave., Chicago, IL 60604–4305. Data on the grants and publications discussed in the next few pages were made available by Barbara Page Fiske, who has been active since the inception of CIS in a number of executive and editorial capacities.

2. The strategic framework is presented as The Movement Action Plan of the Social Movement Empowerment Project, 721 Shrader Street, San Francisco, CA 94117, and is published in the *Dandelion* (Spring 1987), available from the Movement For A New Society, P.O. Box 1922, Cambridge, MA 02238.

3. Michael S. Clark, *Soundings: A Regional Survey* (Seattle, Wash.: Territory Resource, 221 Lloyd Building, Seattle, WA 98101, September 1985), 2.

4. Ibid., 2–3.

5. Ibid., 5–7.

6. Ibid., 8.

7. Ibid., 6–7.

8. Western States Center, *Newsletter* (Winter 1989): 1. Available from the Western States Center, 522 SW 5th Ave., Portland, OR 97204.

Chapter 11

1. John R. Commons, *Institutional Economics: Its Place in Political Economy* (New York: Macmillan, 1934).

2. The political climate affecting foundations with respect to tax legislation is particularly well reported chronologically in Andrews, *Foundation Watcher*. More technical analyses of the various acts are found

in Odendahl, *America's Wealthy*, Chapter 3, "Congress and Foundations" by John A. Edie. The various tax acts are analyzed in Appendix
A of the book, 286ff (Revenue Acts of 1950, 1954, and 1964; the Tax
Reform Act of 1969, and recent legislation: the Marital Deduction Act
of 1982. Also discussed are alternatives to private foundations: public
charities, private operating foundations, exempt operating foundations,
community foundations, split-interest trusts, and pooled income
funds.) Still useful, according to practicing attorneys, is Irwin J. Borof,
"Escaping the Perils of Private Foundation Status," *Economic Development and Law Center Report* (Winter 1981): 43–48.

    3. Coffin, "Justice, Not Charity," 37.

    4. DJB Foundation, *Report*, 7.

    5. One text prepared for funders following the attempt in 1983–1984
by the IRS to get approval of Circular A–122 was *Non-Profit Organiza-
tions, Public Policy, and the Political Process: A Guide to the Internal Revenue
Code and Federal Election Campaign Act* (December 1987), sponsored by
Citizens Vote. It was prepared in the Washington, D.C. law offices of
Perkins Cole by Robert F. Bauer, B. Holly Schadler, and Judith L.
Corley, with review and comment by Gail Harmon of Harmon & Weiss.
It was funded by Belden Fund, the Field Foundation, the New World
Foundation, the Villers Foundation, Windom Fund, and the Youth
Project. For a review of the situation following the 1988 election, see
Larry Blumenthal, "IRS tones down controversial nonprofit lobbying
regulations: Some sticking points remain," *Non Profit Times* 2, no. 10
(January 1989): 1, 6, 15.

    6. Two important books on the civil rights movement are Richard
Klugar, *Simple Justice* (New York: Random House, 1977) and Taylor
Branch, *Parting The Waters: America in the King Years 1954–63* (New York:
Simon & Schuster, 1988)

    7. Excerpted from pages i and l of its 1988 funding proposal and
page 1 of its 1988 State Profiles. Frank Smith, John Richards, and the
staff of the Youth Project were active in evaluating potential grantees
in the designated states. The proposal noted that the board of directors
that makes the funding decisions ("Together they possess an impressive
amount of public interest experience and a demonstrated commitment
to participatory government" [p. 5]) was composed at the time of the
following individuals: Anne Bartley, a director of the Winthrop Rockefeller Foundation and Rockefeller Family Fund and a founding member
of Peace Links; David Cohen, codirector of the Advocacy Institute; Jim
Dyke, an attorney with Hunton Williams; Roberta Greene, director of
development for People for the American Way; Judith Lichtman, executive director of Women's Legal Defense Fund; Patricia Mathews,

vice-president for Public Affairs of the National Bank of Washington; Susan Sechler, director of the Rural Economic Policy program at the Aspen Institute for Humanistic Studies; B. J. Stiles, director of the National Leadership Coalition on AIDS; and Bill Taylor, a Washington lawyer who specializes in civil rights and education issues.

8. Forum Institute, 1988 funding proposal, 3–4.

9. From a USA VOTES memorandum dated November 21, 1988, entitled "Preliminary Review of 1987/88 Program," 1.

10. From a letter from Anne Bartley, president of the Forum Institute, to the Forum's contributors, November 22, 1988, 1.

Chapter 12

1. Bartley to the Forum's contributors, 2.

2. From notes on Tufts Meeting by Don Hazen of *Mother Jones* magazine, as distributed by Common Practice's Harriet Barlow at the Blue Mountain Center (Blue Mountain Lake, New York, NY 12812), December 21, 1988, 1.

3. Ibid., 3. See also, Barbara Ehrenreich, "Rebels Without a Clue," *Zeta* (March 1989): 12–14.

4. Brian O'Connell, president of Independent Sector, wrote an editorial entitled "Already, 1000 Points of Light" to report that millions of people, not thousands, and especially relatively poor people, were volunteering their services and making sizeable contributions to nonprofits (*New York Times*, January 25, 1989, 21). President Bush's "thousand-points-of-light man," Gregg Petersmeyer, is responsible for the new YES (Youth Entering Service) Foundation, with $100 million to expand opportunities for young people to work with existing nonprofit agencies in their communities (*Non Profit Times* 3, no. 1 (April 1989): 10–11). *Business Week* notes the resurgence of social activism in the form of boycotts and initiatives (May 22, 1989, 34), while Salim Muwakkil in *In These Times* writes that black America is apathetic about the social movements that excite white liberals (April 26, 1989, 7).

5. Hazen, *Notes on Tufts*, 4, 9.

6. From notes on " '88 Election Post-mortems: Progressives' Rashomons, Past and Future" by S. M. Miller, as distributed by Common Practice's Harriet Barlow at the Blue Mountain Center (Blue Mountain Lake, New York, NY 12812), December 21, 1988, 3, 6.

7. See for example, Commentary by Karen Pennar, "Why Isn't the Wealth Trickling Down?" *Business Week*, May 1, 1989, 112.

8. Taylor, an experienced social worker spoke to the July 1989 meet-

ing of the Northern Rockies Action Group, of which she is a long-time board member.

9. David Hunter's speech and Waldemar Nielsen's observation about the capture of ideas by the neoconservatives (*Golden Donors*, 40–58) may have been taken to heart. Among the fresh attempts to provide forums for the development of ideas among the kind of people attending the postelection meetings are two newsletters: *The Commonwealth Report* (186 Hampshire Street, Cambridge, MA 02139) and *Democracy Notes* (c/o Richard Healey, 1872 Newton St. NW, Washington, DC 20010). New studies are also being undertaken at the Institute for Policy Studies in Washington, D.C.

10. However, it must be noted that funds organized by women may be an exception to the rule and that the Funding Exchange, under the leadership of Kim Klein, has undertaken to build a $15 million endowment to cover the overhead of its constituent public foundations. In addition, the campaign known as GiveFive to encourage broader individual and corporate giving may help attract new recruits to progressive social change foundations as well as to traditional agencies.

Appendix

1. See also Clark's discussion in Chapter 10 for other comments concerning training of community organizers.

2. For further insight into the ACORN approach, see Gary Delgado, *Organizing the Movement: The Roots and Growth of ACORN*, with Foreword by Richard A. Cloward and Frances Fox Piven (Philadelphia: Temple University Press, 1986).

3. Since these 1987 grants for support of the Progressive Constituency Network, the Youth Project elected to terminate PCN as a continuing project.

Select Bibliography

This is a short, classified, bibliography of important books for readers who wish to delve further into the literature. Almost all of them have been cited in the text or mentioned in the chapter notes (which contain much ephemeral or privately circulated material not listed here). All of them should be currently available in a central library.

The General Field of Philanthropy

The Foundation Center (79 Fifth Ave., New York, NY 10003), working closely with the Council on Foundations and Independent Sector, properly describes itself as the nation's number one source of information on foundation and corporate philanthropy. A score of central libraries across the United States are depositories for its many publications and provide computer access to its files of potential donors. Among its recent books are *Foundations Today* (5th ed., 1988); Robert L. Payton's *The Ethics of Corporate Grant Making* (1987); and, especially, Michael Seltzer's *Securing Your Organization's Future: A Complete Guide to Fundraising Strategies* (1987). Excellent and extensive bibliographies can be found in:

—Freeman, David. *Handbook on Private Foundations.* Cabin John, Md.: Seven Locks Press for the Council on Foundations, 1981.

—Odendahl, Teresa, ed. *America's Wealthy and the Future of Foundations*. New York: Foundation Center, 1987.

Independent Sector (1828 L Street, Washington, DC 20036) has also become a major source of current information about the general nonprofit world and its philanthropic sector. Among its many publications of interest are:

—Hodgkinson, Virginia A., and Murray S. Weitzman. *Dimensions of the Independent Sector: A Statistical Profile*. 2d ed. (1986).

—Also see: "The Charitable Behavior of Americans: Findings from a National Survey" (1986); *Giving and Volunteering in the United States*," for the Daring Goals/Give Five program (1988); *From Belief to Commitment: The Activities and Expenditures of Religious Congregations in the United States* (1988); and Hodgkinson, Virginia A., "Academic Centers and Research Institutes Focusing on the Study of Philanthropy, Voluntarism, and Not-for-Profit Activity: A Progress Report" (November 1988).

"Philanthropy, Patronage, Politics" (special issue), *Daedalus* 116, no. 1 (Winter 1987).

Taft Group. *Fund Raiser's Guide to Religious Philanthropy* and *Fund Raiser's Guide to Private Fortunes*. Washington, D.C.: Taft Group, 1987.

Progressive Social Change Philanthropy

Johnson, Robert Matthews. *The First Charity: How Philanthropy Can Contribute to Democracy in America*. Cabin John, Md.: Seven Locks Press, 1988.

Klein, Kim. *Fundraising for Social Change*. 2d ed. Inverness, Calif.: Chardon Press, 1988.

United States Catholic Conference. *Daring to Seek Justice: People Working Together: The Story of the Campaign for Human Development: Its Roots, Its Programs and Its Challenges*. Washington, D.C.: United States Catholic Conference, 1986.

Vanguard Public Foundation. *Robin Hood Was Right: A Guide to Giving Your Money for Social Change*. San Francisco, Calif.: Vanguard Public Foundation, 1977. An updated edition is forthcoming.

A selected list of directories of progressive social change funders and investors:

—Delgado, Gary. *Activist's Guide to Religious Funders: Leveraging God's Resources from Her Representatives on Earth: A Working Model.* Oakland, Calif.: Center for Third World Organizing, 1987.

—Institute for Community Economics and Funding Exchange. *Directory of Socially Responsible Investments.* 2d ed. New York: Funding Exchange, 1986.

—Public Media Center. *Index of Progressive Funders.* San Francisco, Calif.: Public Media Center, 1985.

—Shellow, Jill R., and Nancy C. Stella, eds. *Grant Seekers Guide: Funding Sourcebook.* 3d rev. ed. Mt. Kisco, N.Y.: Moyer Bell for the National Network of Grantmakers, 1989.

Bauer, Robert F., B. Holly Schadler, and Judith L. Corley, *Non-Profit Organizations, Public Policy, and the Political Process: A Guide to the Internal Revenue Code and Federal Election Campaign Act.* Washington, D.C.: Perkins Coie, Attorneys, 1987. This publication was sponsored by Citizens Vote. See also Blumenthal, Larry. "IRS tones down controversial nonprofit lobbying regulations: Some sticking points remain." *Non Profit Times* 2, no. 10 (January 1989): 1, 6, 15.

Current Insights on Social Change

Boyte, Harry. *Commonwealth of Freedom: The Promise of Citizen Politics.* New York: Free Press, 1989.

Delgado, Gary. *Organizing the Movement: The Roots and Growth of ACORN.* Foreword by Richard A. Cloward and Frances Fox Piven. Philadelphia: Temple University Press, 1986.

Lappe, Frances. *Rediscovering America's Values.* New York: Ballantine Books, 1989.

Raskin, Marcus, and Chester Hartman, eds. *Winning America: Ideas in Leadership for the 1990's.* Boston, Mass.: South End Press and the Institute for Policy Studies, 1988. The address of the Institute for Policy Studies is 1601 Connecticut Avenue, NW, Washington, D.C. 20009.

Two newsletters: *The Commonwealth Report* (186 Hampshire Street, Cambridge, MA 02139) and *Democracy Notes* (c/o Richard Healey, 1872 Newton St. NW, Washington, DC 20010).

Characteristics of Funders

Aldrich, Nelson W., Jr. *Old Money: The Mythology of America's Upper Class*. New York: Knopf, 1988.

Hochschild, Adam. *Half the Way Home: A Memoir of Father and Son*. New York: Penguin Books, 1987.

Schervish, Paul G., and Andrew Herman. *The Study on Wealth and Philanthropy: Final Report*. Chestnut Hill, Mass.: Social Welfare Research Institute, Boston College, 1988.

History of Philanthropy

Andrews, F. Emerson. *Foundation Watcher*. Lancaster, Pa.: Princeton University Press, 1973.

Commission on Foundations. *Commission on Foundations: Private Giving and Public Policy*. Chicago: University of Chicago Press, 1971.

Heimann, Fritz, ed. *The Future of Foundations*. Englewood Cliffs, N.J.: Prentice-Hall for the American Assembly, Columbia University, 1973.

Hulseman, Bertha F. *American Foundations for Social Welfare*. New York: Russell Sage Foundation, 1938.

Merrill, Charles. *The Checkbook: The Politics and Ethics of Foundation Philanthropy*. Boston, Mass.: Oelgeschlager, Gunn & Hain, 1986.

Nielsen, Waldemar. *The Big Foundations*. New York: Columbia University, 1972.

Nielsen, Waldemar. *The Golden Donors*. New York: Truman Talley Books, 1985.

Pifer, Alan J. *Reflections on Thirty Years*. New York: Council on Foundations, 1984.

Social History

Branch, Taylor. *Parting the Waters: America in the King Years 1954–63*. New York: Simon & Schuster, 1988.

Commons, John R. *Institutional Economics: Its Place in Political Economy*. New York: Macmillan, 1934.

Hofstadter, Richard. *Social Darwinism in American Thought*. Boston: Beacon Press, 1955.

Klugar, Richard. *Simple Justice*. New York: Random House, 1977.

Index

Abelard Foundation, 49
Accountability: of funders, 112; of grantees, 104
ACORN, 50, 147; grants for, 174
Administration of the granted funds, 105
Aldrich, Nelson W., Jr., 59
Alinsky, Saul, 46, 76, 117
American Civil Liberties Union, 42
America's Wealthy and the Future of Foundations, 29, 59–60
Andrews, F. Emerson, 38
ARCA Foundation, 50
Asian groups, grants for, 184
A Territory Resource Foundation (ATR), 61, 73, 121–26

Babcock Foundation, Mary Reynolds, 76

Baldwin, Roger, 42
Barlow, Harriet, 146
Bay Area Committee for Responsive Philanthropy, 7, 14
Belden Fund, 49
Bernstein, Daniel J. *See* DJB Foundation
Black organizations, grants for, 168
Bok, Derek, 54
Bookbinder, Hyman, 110
Boone, Dick, 49
Booth, Heather, 50, 76
Bothwell, Robert, 40
Boyte, Harry, 205 n.4
Bush, George, 73, 147
Business-related foundations, 137

Cagen, Leslie, 147
Campaign for Human Develop-

ment, 57–59, 83, 100, 112, 150;
criteria used, 73–79; granting
patterns, 87, 158; history of,
57; investments in socially re-
sponsible firms, 22
Carnegie Foundation, 40
Carson, Rachel, 40
Center for Community Change,
40, 49, 127
Center for Third World Organiz-
ing (CTWO), 50, 127, 146, 163
CHD. *See* Campaign for Human
Development
Children, youth, and families,
grants for, 52
Churches and religious organiza-
tions, 18; funding by, 124
Citizen participation, 140, 145
Citizens' Action movement, 139
Citizens Information Service,
117–20
Civil Rights Act of 1964, 46, 139
Clark, Michael S., 121–26
Coffin, Rev. William Sloane, 54,
137, 150
Commission on Private Philan-
thropy and Public Needs, 40
Commons, John R., 135
Community-based organizations.
See Grass-roots organizations
Community foundations, 18, 66.
See also Foundations, private
Community organizing. *See*
Grass-roots organizing
Congressional investigations of
foundations, 39, 136
Conway, Lenny, 49
Corporate charitable foundation,
18, 54, 65; links to firms, 137.
See also Foundations, private
Cost-benefit analysis, 109
Council on Foundations, 15, 20
Council on National Priorities,
51, 64, 93

Criteria, funding, 73–79, 101. *See
also* Evaluation
Critical thinking and education,
154
C. S. Fund/Maryanne Mott Charitable Trust, 67

Data Center, The, 22
Delgado, Gary, 50
Democrats, 133, 146
de Toqueville, Alexis, 135
Direct support of service provid-
ers, 30, 78
DJB Foundation, 46, 60, 74, 116,
137
Donor-advised funds, 19
Dunbar, Leslie, 46

Economic justice, 53, 82, 150
Economic security and develop-
ment, 82
Eisenberg, Pablo, 50
Elections, 139, 145–50
Electoral politics, 139
Empowerment as basis for social
change activism, 61, 121, 150
Entitlements, 10
Environmental concerns and tox-
ics, 82; grants concerning, 194
Evaluation: of funders, 113; of
grants and grantees, 99–107; of
social change philanthropy,
109, 113; subjectivity in, 103

Family foundations. *See* Founda-
tions, private
Farm crisis, grants concerning,
186
Federal government, responsibil-
ities and programs, 43, 104
Federal income tax. *See* Internal
Revenue Service; Tax Reform

Act of 1969; Tax Reform Act of 1986

Field Foundation, 44, 116, 120, 148

Fileno, Edward A., 38

Filer, John, 72

Financial analysis: of grantees, 105; of grants, 101

Finks, David, 76

Fiske, Barbara Page, 118

Ford Foundation, 28, 39, 118

Forum Institute, 140–43, 145

Foundation Center, 15, 95

Foundation Directory, 29

Foundations, private, 27, 39, 66, 124, 137; early ("great"), 38, 135; large endowed, 28, 41, 87, 153; and public affairs, 41; and social activism, 38. *See also* Foundations, public; Philanthropy in U.S.

Foundations, public, 18, 19, 31, 66, 137

Friedmann, John, 43

Funders: evaluation of granting work, 109–16; relation to grantees, 117, 124

Funders Committee on Voter Registration and Education, 140

Funding Exchange, 19, 31, 51, 64, 87, 122

Funding for social change: criteria and guidelines, 73–79; funding decisions and funding cycle, 99–107, 126; fund-raising, 124, 153; funds estimated for support of, 30–33. *See also* Evaluation; Grantees; Philanthropy in U.S.; Social change philanthropy

Gap between rich and poor, 53, 150

Gardner, John, 41

Garland, Charles, 42

Get-out-the-vote (GOTV) campaigns, 139, 150

Goldmark, Peter C., 41

Grantees: defined, 73–79, 81–83; finances, 123; functions performed, 81; relation to funders, 117–24; survivability, 121–23

Grants for social change: distribution by subject, race, state, 84–85; sample analyzed, 83–96. *See also* Funding for social change; Social change grantees; Social change philanthropy

Grantseekers Guide, 65

Grass-roots organizations, as grantees, 18, 78, 104, 124

Grass-roots organizing, 50, 82, 138, 149; grants for, 159

Great Society programs, 46, 104

Greene, Jerome D., 41

Greying of Sixties activists, 125, 153

Guidelines, funding, 73–79, 101

Hahn, Kurt, 56

Harrington, Michael, 45

Hart, Jeffrey, 39

Hartman, Chester, 93

Harvard Business School, 136

Haymarket People's Fund, 19, 49

Hazen, Don, 146–48

Health, education, and welfare, grants concerning, 196

Heilbroner, Robert F., 9

Herman, Andrew, 61

Highlander Center (and Folk School), 45, 129, 152

Hispanic organizations, grants for, 178

Hochschild, Adam, 59
Housing and community development, grants for, 81, 192
Hunter, David R., 46, 113, 152

Independent Sector, 15, 25; on religious funders, 53
Individuals as funders, 15, 18
Institute for Community Economics, 23
Institute for Policy Studies, 50, 93
Institutional change, 77, 115, 137
Interfaith Center on Corporate Responsibility, 22
Internal Revenue Service, 15, 138, 155. *See also* Tax code; Tax Reform Act of 1969; Tax Reform Act of 1986
Investing, socially responsible, 22

Jacobson, Joy, 142
Jenkins, J. Craig, 30, 46
Jewish Fund for Justice, 76
Johnson, Robert Mathews, 7, 13, 54, 83, 100
Joint Foundation Support, 84
Joyce Foundation, 49, 120
Judis, John B., 10
Junk mail, 138

Kahn, Si, 50
Kaplan Fund, J. M., 49
Kennedy, Robert F., 40
Keppel, Frederick P., 40
Kest, Steve, 50
Klein, Kim, 7
Knowles, Louis, 76
Kristol, Irving, 40

Lappe, Frances Moore, 205 n.4
Liberals, 133
Lyman, Richard, 4

McCarthy, Sen. Joseph, 135
MacKaye, Benton, 43
Malachowsky, Jeff, 128
Malone, Rev. James W., 57
Media projects, grants for, 201
Merrill, Charles, 106, 111
Midwest Academy, 50, 152
Miller, S. M., 146, 148–50
Mitchell, Bill, 50
Montana Alliance for Progressive Politics, 139
Mott family funds, 49, 67–69
Ms. Foundation for Women, 66
Myrdal, Gunnar, 40

National Association for the Advancement of Colored People (NAACP), 42
National Center for Charitable Statistics, 17
National Center for Responsive Philanthropy, 14, 50
National Committee for Responsible Philanthropy, 54
National Conference for Catholic Bishops. *See* Campaign for Human Development
National economic revitalization, grants concerning, 188
National Network for Grantmakers, 51, 93, 113
National Network of Women's Funds, 51
National Taxonomy of Exempt Entities (NTEE), 17, 82
Native American organizations, grants for, 163
Needmor Fund, 49
Networking by progressive funders, 37, 50, 90
New Deal, 42–44
New donors, 153–54

New World Foundation, 46, 49, 94

Nielsen, Waldemar, 40, 111

Norman Foundation, 49, 140

Northern Rockies Action Group (NRAG), 127, 152

Organizing, community. *See* Grass-roots organizing

Ottinger Foundation, 49

Outward Bound School, 54

PACs (political action committees), 138

Partnership for Democracy. *See* Youth Project

Patman, Rep. Wright, 39, 135. *See also* Congressional investigations of foundations

Peace, national security, and arms control, grants for, 82, 200

Pennick, George, 76

Peterson Commission, 40

Philanthropy in U.S.: church-related funding, 31, 124; flow of funds, 25; goals, 9; policies, 13; structure of, 16. *See also* Foundations, private; Social change philanthropy

Pike, Drummond, 50, 101, 119

Political action in the U.S., 133, 138

Political education, 148

Political implications of grants, 133

Populist movement, 135

Private foundations. *See* Foundations, private

Progressive constituency and movement, 127, 133, 135, 145; agenda, 148; grants to help build, 202

Progressive Constituency Network, 51, 203

Progressive social change grants, 81–96. *See also* Social change philanthropy

Public foundations, 18, 19, 31, 66, 137

Public Media Center, 65

Public-policy or issues research, 40–41, 81, 114

Ramage, David, 46

Raskin, Marcus, 93

Rathke, Wade, 50

Religious traditions as basis for activism, 53–58

Republicans, 133

Research projects, 81, 114, 152

Richards, John, 40

Riessman, Frank, 146

Rightists, 5, 15, 114

Risk analysis and the funding decision, 99–107. *See also* Evaluation

Rockefeller philanthropies, 28, 41, 49, 69

Roisman, Lois, 76

Rosenwald Foundation, Julius, 44

Russell Sage Foundation, 38

Ruth Mott Fund, 67

Sacks, Albert M., 38

Sanchez, Frank, 50

Schervish, Paul, 61

Schools and public education, 82

Schumpeter, Joseph, 9

Schwartzhaupt Foundation, 44, 118

Seventh Generation Fund, 66, 163

Shalon Foundation, 49

Simon, John, 38

Site visits in granting, 102–3
Smith, Frank, 140
Social change grantees: defined, 8, 73–79; examples of, 157–204; typology and analysis of, 81–96. *See also* Grantees; Grants for social change
Social change philanthropy: defined, 14, 73–79; funders profiled, 19; funding, 37, 83–96; future of, 115; policies exemplified, 46–49. *See also* Philanthropy in U.S.
Social Darwinism, 54
Social logics of the wealthy, 62–64
Socially responsible investing, 22
Social Movement Enpowerment Project, 121
Social movements in the U.S., 37, 53, 114
Social Trends, 53
Social Venture Network, 23
Southern economic conditions, grants to improve, 185
Southwest Voter Registration Project, 50
Staffs of foundations, 20, 46, 60, 100, 125
Stein, Rob, 142
Stern Fund, 46, 49, 116
Surveys of wealthy donors, 59–69
Symbiosis between funder and grantee, 124

Tabankin, Margery, 50
Taconic Foundation, 49
Tax code: Section 501(c)(3) organizations, 16, 26, 105, 137; Section 501(c)(4) "lobbying" groups, 137; Section 4945f organizations, 137

Tax-exempt status, 105, 136. *See also* Tax code
Tax liabilities of grantees, 101
Tax Reform Act of 1969, 39, 136
Tax Reform Act of 1986, 4, 88
Taylor, Nancy, 151
Technical assistance grants, 127
Think tanks, 18, 105, 138, 150
Thousand points of light, 73, 147
Threshold Foundation, 51, 64, 84
Tides Foundation, 20, 49, 84
Training institutes, 152

United Way, 8, 26
USA VOTES, 222, 226

Vanguard Public Foundation, 19, 49, 64
Veatch program (North Shore Unitarian Universalist Society), 95
Veblen, Thorsten, 135
Velasquez, Willie, 50, 147
Voter registration and get-out-the-vote (GOTV) campaigns, 139; grants for, 198

Wealth, empowerment, and freedom of choice, 61
Wealthy individuals and philanthropy, studies of, 29, 59–64
Western States Center, 128
Wieboldt Foundation, 8, 118
Women's economic status, grants concerning, 191
Women's Foundation, 84
Women's funding organizations, potential, 154
Women's rights, grants concerning, 196
Worker-owned or cooperative businesses, 11, 78

Yale study, 29, 59
Younger group of wealthy indi-
  viduals, 60, 125
Youth Project (public founda-

tion), 19, 20, 46, 49, 50, 84,
  105, 127, 140

Zevin, Robert, 220

About the Author

ALAN RABINOWITZ has been active in the field of social change philanthropy for two decades. He is a consultant on urban land economics, state/local finance, and real estate markets and a former Professor of Urban Planning at the University of Washington. Among his previous books is *Land Investment and the Predevelopment Process* (Quorum, 1988).